BACKSTREETS

Living in My Truck & Out of My Head

PETER F. GROOVES

With special thanks to:
Editor: Jesse Schwartz
Cover Design: Dillon Glenn
Author Profile Photography: Wesley Horbatuck IV

ISBN 9781095833759
Independently published

For Mama, Dads, and The Gin Bandits

CONTENTS

1

ROUTE AROUND

(1:13)

I walked out to my truck that morning, same as a hundred mornings before it. With my flip flops still slightly damp from the gym shower and my chest a little sore from my workout, I exchanged pleasantries with Mary at the front desk and strolled through the parking lot towards my home. Once I got there, I took out my key chain and used one key to unlock the shell and another to unlock the tailgate. Once the shell was unlocked, I flipped open the latch and then dropped down the tailgate to get to my closet, where I kept all of my clothes and necessities. I would typically close the shell hatch once the tailgate was dropped so that I could get into all of the contents in the drawers I had built underneath my bed without leaving the bed area open for people to look in and judge. For whatever reason, I didn't do that this day, leaving my bedroom open for the world to see.

At this point, I had been living in my truck for four months. I had most of my routine down to a science. Wake up, roll out of the back, drive to the gym eating a protein bar on the way, pack my trusty backpack with my work clothes and gym outfit, workout, shower and change for work. If you read that sentence subtracting the "roll out of my truck" bit, it sounds like a pretty normal 25 year old guy's morning.

The morning gym routine is something that I had always wanted to commit to, but never had the willpower to keep it going. I was the guy that would wake up with my head running a thousand miles a minute thinking of excuses for why I should let myself go back to sleep. "I am a little sick, I should probably let myself recover;" "I'll just go after work;" Or "I'll just do twice as much tomorrow." Basically, I was just being a hack and not having any strength of mind. One of my all time favorite quotes is by a scientist named Tim Noakes that goes, "the winner is the athlete to whom defeat is the least acceptable rationalization" (McCluskey, p. 160).[1] Meaning in my case: if you're a winner, you'll do everything conceivable to not make those excuses and just wake up and do your workout, starting your day with your first win. I didn't just want to stop making the excuses. I wanted to eliminate the possibility of them altogether.

When I lived in a house, I rationalized defeat like "Defeat Rationalizer" was the title on my business card. Honest to god, one of the main reasons I moved into the truck was to stop rationalizing defeat. I had no other choice but to go to the gym each and every morning. Well, I guess the other choice would be to go into work smelling like butt checks and risk getting fired, but to me that wasn't much of a choice. Where else was I going to shower?

So that was exactly what I did. I went to the gym every morning and if I was going, I was working out. Somebody asked me if I ever just went to shower and I said that if I ever did that, I would move out of the truck because that would be the weakest decision imaginable. My buddy once told me about a girl he went to college with that he watched run around the corner of these buildings, where she thought nobody could see her. Once she thought she was out of sight, she talked on the phone for thirty minutes, dumped water on her head and ran the same 100 yards back to her sorority house to let everyone know she was running. Long story short, if I was going to be living in my truck to help motivate me into getting into shape, the last thing that I was going to do was cheat it.

Let me clarify one thing. I am by no means a meathead. I am 5'8 and weighed a buck fifty sopping wet. The point is, I was trying to get bigger and I needed to put in the work to get there. This may be a drastic step and was far from the only reason, but it made all of my excuses go away.

Once I started going, I wondered how I ever started my day without it. I was more productive at work, felt more accomplished all throughout the day and was sleeping much better. I was getting more toned by the week and feeling more confident in myself. Again, I had no excuse not to go and had to go if I wanted to not be the asshole that stinks up the surrounding cubicles. But the more I went, the less it felt like a chore and the more it felt like something I needed to do to keep me moving forward in my life.

So anyways, I pull out my drawers starting to put my dirty gym clothes in the designated dirty laundry drawer that I had built into the "bed frame" (also known as the wooden dresser I had built that my mattress pad rested on top of and drawers that contained all of my clothes, but I'll get into that more later). Once I put the dirties away, I put my damp shower sandals into the sides between the bed frame and the truck bed frame, where I keep all of my shoes. Then I'd pick one of my work shoes out and grab a pair of socks and put those on.

As I'm doing all of this I look to my right and see this kid around my age doing a very similar routine across the parking lot. Our tail lights were facing each other, meaning our bedroom doors were open and you could see into one from the other. He had a Toyota Tundra, practically putting on the dog compared to my little Tacoma. And guess what: all of his shit was in some plastic bins under a wooden "bed frame" with a mattress pad on top. In my honest opinion, my setup was slightly better as I had him beat in the bed width, curtains, and drawers departments. His bed was about the width of a twin, and mine was closer to a double, but he may have had some other use for the spare space that I couldn't see from my neighborly perspective. He had me beat, however on the bed length and bed thickness departments, so it wasn't a blowout of a competition by any means. His mattress pad looked like one of those ones that the richest kid on your dorm hall had, the one that was about 6 inches thick and felt like you were laying on a pile of clouds. If I had that one in my Tacoma, my face would be even closer to the ceiling and I didn't have much room to spare as it was. But I'm not here to play Extreme Makeover: Home Toyota Edition. More than anything else, I was fucking stoked to see another kid like me doing it.

He was wearing stylish clothes and the Tundra looked like a 2016 or newer (it's 2018 as I write this) and he didn't have a beard down to his feet or disgusting teeth. He looked like a guy that would be in my friend group. I'm also not here to play the Bachelorette and tell you about who the smoke guys are at the gym driving expensive trucks. I wouldn't give a shit if his teeth were fucked up or if he was wearing Skechers shoes and an Old Navy t-shirt. The fact that he was stylish, well groomed and in a new truck just proved one thing to me. He wasn't doing this to get out of debt. He wasn't doing this because he was out of a job. Most importantly, he wasn't doing this out of need, but out of want. He was choosing to live like this, just as I was.

There were a lot of reasons people were choosing to live like this and I couldn't sum it up any better than Lucy Feldman did in *TIME* magazine:

> The meaning of van life is up for debate: Depending who you ask, you might get a practical or an existential answer. To some, living in a van is about living minimally, akin to the obsession with tiny houses or the Marie Kondo method of tidying up, but on wheels. Or it's a direct response to the housing crisis, a way to reduce the cost of living or a push against the pull of corporate life — Nomadland, a new book from journalist Jessica Bruder, follows retirees who've traded their houses for homes on wheels that can carry them where odd jobs can keep them afloat. To others, van life is a means to an end, where the end is more time spent hiking, rock climbing, kayaking, hanging with your dog or your partner, sipping stovetop coffee on the beach at sunrise. It's about waking up wherever you want, doing whatever you want, moving on whenever you want. "The big thing," says Brianna Madia, 27, who lives with her husband in a 1990 Ford E350, "is recognizing how little you need to be happy" (Feldman, 2017).[2]

Maybe he was running from something, or wanted to travel more, or wanted to force himself out of his comfort zone to find out things about himself he never knew. Or maybe he had his other reasons for living a minimalist lifestyle that were completely different than mine. I'm sure he wasn't living in a community of people living like me and him. He surely had friends that were living in homes or apartments that thought what he was doing was crazy. The fact was that he was saying "screw what everyone else sees as normal. I'm doing this because that's what I want to do."

I felt that way wholeheartedly. I knew from the start that people would think it was weird. I knew that people would make fun of me. I knew that I would have to explain to people that would never understand, but much more than this, I knew that what I was doing was what I believed in my heart was the best course of action for me, and what everyone else thought was just going to be what they thought.

The life on the road/van life/vehicle living/wheel estate movement is much bigger than most people realize. According to the *San Diego Union Tribune*, the cost of shelter for millions of households was at least half of their incomes, so a lot of people have started to look at car payments more like a less expensive rent payment (Reed, 2017).[3] For me, the car was already being paid for anyways, so the rent was basically free.

I understand that a lot of people have different circumstances than my own. Most people that are living in their vehicles are doing so to make ends meet or to get them through a tough time while trying to get back on their feet. I empathize with those people and always have. My parents couldn't even take me into the cities growing up because I would get so upset seeing homeless people. Now I was one of those homeless people, but just a different type of homeless.

I aim to talk more about my type of homeless, or as I'd like to put it, "alternatively homed." There were plenty of people like me out there too. As soon as I started thinking about wanting to do this, I would see more and more of the Westfalia vans or converted school buses, or vans that people had built out to live in. Just like when you think that you want to get a certain type of car or find out that the girl you have a crush on drives a certain type of car, you see it like it's every other car. The more I talked to people about doing it, the more I would hear "oh I have a friend that does that," or, "my brother actually did that for a while," or "I'm actually living on a small sailboat right now docked in the bay." It seemed like there were a lot of people that were downsizing or living on the road and those people also had all of their teeth and seemed like they had their shit together.

It was true, van sales were up, and not like your mother's minivan. I mean vans like Sprinter Vans that were commonly used for converted living. RV lots were getting more and more crowded, and with younger people too. The tiny home, van life, and anything of the like was becoming something that didn't sound as crazy as it once did (Feldman, 2017).[2] Hashtag vanlife was growing and growing in a big way.

Big time successes had tried out this little experiment at one time or another, too. The CEO of my company lived in a van, working on a farm, when he came up with the a-ha moment to start his own company using a sustainable building product he worked directly with on that farm. Jack Johnson lived in a van with his future wife for a bit while he was travelling and that is mostly what the song "I Got You" is about. Even Hollywood heartthrob Chris Pratt lived in a van for a little bit just trying to make enough money for food and fishing supplies (Weisman).[4] It seemed like all of these big time successes had it figured out back then. They wanted to live simple lives with people they cared about, spending most of their time doing what they loved.

The phenomenon was as common as 15,000 people living in vehicles in Los Angeles alone in a recent study (Hoffower, 2018).[5] I'm sure that a large percentage of those people were doing it out of necessity. Let's just assume that only 10% of those people weren't doing it out of need. That's still 1,500 people in one city alone. Of those 1,500, I am sure that some were the type of van lifers that travel from town to town and work freelance or remote jobs where they could work anywhere that there is Wifi. Honestly, this was the ultimate dream, but at that time in my life, those weren't my circumstances. I had a solid job that I wasn't ready and couldn't afford to lose, and I honestly couldn't think of a better town in the world than San Diego to live in. I was happy to stay where I was, but travel from place to place on the weekends and get outside more to enjoy the finest city in America during the week. I wasn't sure how many people of the 15,000 in L.A. living in their vehicles were like me, working a desk job but living a double life outside of the office. In San Diego, I knew there was at least one other.

This guy standing at the truck next door was more than just another van life, minimalist buddy. He was vindication. He was living proof that there were more people out there living like me and damn happy doing it. I looked over at him just as he caught me checking out his wheel estate and he checked out mine, and I said "My man."

He looked over at me, as we both fought back these shit eating grins as if we had just gotten away with a high school prank, laughed and cheerfully said, "what's up brother?" With that, everything that was needed to be said between us was said and we both started chuckling, hopped into our mobile homes and headed on with our normal lives.

2

CABIN BY THE SEA

(0:36)

Banks and I were done with the beach for the day, so we decided to head back to our little beach house that we had rented with three of our other buddies for the summer of 2012. You'd walk into this house and immediately get hit with this smell. No, not a smell actually – a stench. A smell leaves room for doubt that the smell could have been a positive thing. Everyone knows when you say "stench" that it is going to be something with some stank. I like to believe it was stuck into the disgusting, thirty year old shag carpets, and not us, because the place smelled that way when we got there. We really didn't help the cause, though. The house had a kitchen connected with a decently sized living room with an L-shaped couch. The stove was the only real separator of to the two rooms. Whenever someone said, "I'm in the kitchen" it really just meant they were in the south end of the living room. Then, to the left as you walked in there were two bedrooms and one bathroom for five fellas.

Banks and I had the double bedroom that was about the width of a king sized bed and the length of a little bit more than that. The only furniture was one dresser and a bunk bed. Johnny and the two Jordan's lived in the other room that wasn't much bigger, with even less room to operate for three people. Banks and I basically got the master suite. Six years later, I can picture every inch of that room, not that there were a lot of inches to picture. Banksy and I would treat that place like we had all the room in the world, leaving our clothes all over the floor as if we could afford the space. At times, you couldn't even see the carpet. Quarters were tight, but I'd never loved a room more.

The bathroom was something else. It was tiny and had five guys emptying in it, so you do the math. But, the best part about that bathroom was the day Banks came out into the living room and told us that he had clogged the toilet. We didn't have a plunger, so what ole Banksy did next was matched only in its disgustingness by its resourcefulness. He duct taped two plastic knives together, used his shirt as a mask over his face like a surgeon so that he could withstand the stink and... took care of the clog. We were the definitions of beach bums.

So after the beach, Banks and I walked into the house and it was just the two of us, as it had been many afternoons after we had quit our summer jobs at Hooters. Hooters was the best and worst job I ever had. It is by far the job that I think about the most and the one that gave me the most laughs, but also the job that pissed me off the most. Banks started a couple days earlier than me and when he got home that day, he walked into the house without saying a word, slammed down a pack of cigarettes and walked out onto the back porch to smoke one. I remember thinking, "Jesus, how bad could it have been?" I'd never seen him buy a pack, so I knew the first day was ass. And my first day was ass too.

My first day there was the busiest day in Hooters history, literally. It made more revenue in one day than any Hooters in the history of Hooters. And there was young PFG in the back of the house scrubbing dishes for 16 goddamn hours. I'd fill up a tray of dishes, spray them with the hose, put 'em in the industrial sized dish washer, *BOOM* slam the lever down to let the dishwasher do its deed, and by the time I'd look back there would be twice as many dishes piled up as before. It was hell.

The back of the house was the worst job, by far. After a couple weeks, we moved our way out of there and into the kitchen working fry side and make up. It was tough work, but we were fucking around a decent amount, slipping each other boneless wings from fry side (Banks to me) or tots from make up (me to Banks), and shooting the shit with the Hooters waitresses. Like I said, it was the *best* and worst job that I ever had.

Going in there, we pretended like we were going into war. When we'd get back from the beach in the morning, one of us would make himself and the other guy a fluffernutter. We always made them Willy Wonka style: that's when you put the pieces of bread facing the opposite directions like the grandparents slept in Willy Wonka. And with Kitty Litter: that's when you put chips inside of the sandwich. Meanwhile, the other guy would shower and then get the shit ready for the shift while the other guy showered. We'd get to the Hooters, walk to the door and always say the same things. One would say, "Happy hunting" and the other would respond, "Always trying to get home." We'd give each other a pound and then walk in absolutely mentally psyched for the day. I get chills even typing it, no kidding.

We'd work hard for ten hours-ish, and then as soon as our manager said we could go, and sometimes before, we were SPRINTING out of there. And I mean sprinting. We'd walk out to the main door and as soon as those doors closed, it was a dead sprint like we were trying to escape North Korea, praying that our manager wouldn't think of one more thing to do and shout, "Hey wait, someone's gotta change the sign!" We were always out of the parking lot before that could happen. We'd get home, and on the best days, all of our buddies would already be at our place boozing and we'd run into the house, rip off our flour-soaked Hooters t-shirts, jump into the shower, rinse off in the shower for two minutes, and join the party wearing nothing but board shorts and a tank, if any shirt. No shoes, ever.

It was a good life, but what was to follow was the best life. We got another job at a place called the Crab Cakes Machine. The guy told us we had the jobs and we felt like we could quit our gigs at Hooters, so that was what we decided to do. When we took the original Hooters interview, the manager asked the three of us (our other roommate, Jordan worked there in the mornings), "If one of you quits, the others won't, right?" and we looked her dead in the eye and said "No, no, no of course not, that's not us." I, by, no means consider myself a quitter and I know that Banks isn't either, so we honestly probably believed that we weren't going to just up and quit together. But that is exactly what we did when we thought we had new jobs.

We just quit like cowards. I had gotten back from the beach and showered, made my sando and got ready solo. Banks was at the doctor that morning and as I was leaving, he was pulling in. I immediately U-turned and went back to the house.

"It's a prime beach day," I pleaded, telling him the truth of the unreal day out there in the sand and in the waves. "We can't go in today."

We went back and forth on if we should go or not for a couple minutes and then just decided we would let fate decide. We were going to flip a coin. Tails, we would put our heads down, keep working hard until we had a true last day hoorah before our first day at Crab Cakes Machine. Heads, we would quit our jobs at Hooters, turn our phones off, walk to the beach, have an absolutely phenomenal day in the water, and never look back. It was heads.

What followed was one of the biggest blessings in disguise that had ever happened to me. It was a few days after the day of the coin flip when we decided it was time to text our "new boss" over at Crab Cakes Machine, or as he is still saved in my phone to this day, "Ccm."

"Hey, what day do you want us to start working?"

"Idk, not busy enough 2 give hrs just now.. Sorry"

"Okay, thanks for getting back to me. When do you think you will need more people?"

"I hope that happens right now! Lol"

It was the least professional conversation I would ever have with a "boss" and it turned out that they never got busy enough and this guy, who told us we could quit our jobs because we had other jobs lined up there, never gave us those jobs. So, Banks and I were out of work, living at the beach after our freshman years of college, with enough money from our Hooters stash to get by for the rest of the summer, but we were really *just* getting by.

We had enough money for Special K bar breakfasts, PB&J lunches, and Ramen or Wal Mart burger dinners on repeat with the rest of the money being fivers going toward the beer run or toward kegs for parties at our little shack that felt like a palace. We were waking up, hitting the beach for hours, coming back to the house to watch some tube or play some cards or grill out back, and then either going to a party at one of our buddies' places or having one of our own once the working folk got off. If anyone ever wanted to buddy, Banks and I were there. If anybody ever wanted a body surfing buddy Banks and I were there. And if anybody ever wanted a drinking buddy, Banks and I were definitely there.

Which brings me back to that hot summer day that we walked into the house just the two of us. We had some leftover beers in the fridge from the night before and decided to drink a couple and watch the movie *Art of Flight*. If anyone hasn't seen the movie, it's about this legendary snowboarder taking a trip with some of his buddies around the world hitting some of the most insane mountains on Earth. The movie has the most bumping soundtrack, so it is bound to just get you jacked up. By the end of it, that is exactly what Banks and I were, jacked the fuck up.

We were so jacked up, in fact, that we decided to go shotgun beers on our back porch. We headed back there, screamed some nonsense, and pierced our Natty Lights with keys, turned them upright and down the hatch they went. We were so fired up after one, we did a second... and a third. This was the most quintessential day in the life of Banks and PFG, unemployed at the beach. Getting hyped up on something after a day at the beach and boozing in celebration as if we had just won the Super Bowl. Goddamn, life was good.

I was lucky enough to see Bruce Springsteen on Broadway during the time that I lived in my truck, and he talked about this idea of being absolutely happy when he had "nothing." He was laying on a couch in the back of a pickup truck with the smell of saltwater passing through his nose and he thought to

14

himself that he had it all right then. He paused and said that maybe he did. That line stuck with me more than any in the entire production. It brought me back to that summer when I was living that beach bum life and having nothing and having it all at the same damn time.

That summer was really my first taste of not needing a lot to get the most out of life. To be clear, I am not saying boozing and watching movies is "getting the most out of life." What I mean, was not necessarily the lifestyle, but the mindset. We were the happiest when we really had no money, weren't buying fancy meals or nice new clothes, but instead we were living off of the scraps that we would get from Costco and sandwiches we could whip up for about $3 a day and wearing nothing but our board shorts at all times.

Our energy was contagious and anytime our buddies would come down to the beach, you could see the happiness in them too. We were all living our best life. This was never more evident than the following weekend when the other boys came down to visit. Johnny took off work and joined us as we invented our own version of a game he played in college, Dunkaroos. Essentially, their game was someone would hold you up by the feet while you plunged your head into ice cold water before coming up to shotgun a beer. What we did, being the boys we were and loving competition, was turn it into a game between two teams of two. One guy would dunk his head into the bucket of ice water while his teammate was chugging his beer. When one of the teammates either couldn't chug or withstand the cold of the tub any longer, they would switch until both beers were finished. The rules were you could not drink unless your teammate's whole head was under the water. We played all day. You'd come up out of that bucket, half in a haze of confusion from the cold, chug your beer and then go back to taking the plunge.

The buckets were left outside on the porch and we ended up having a party that night. After a few more beers, people thought it was a smart idea to go out and play on the porch around midnight. The cops were called, one of my buddies was cited, but of all the parties we had at our house, this was by far the most electric. I still have never seen chicks have as fun of a time doing anything as they did dunking their heads into this dirty water that we had been playing with all day, chugging shitty beers. We were all good kids from nice neighborhoods, going to respected universities with strong ambitions for life. But after our freshman years, the best times we could find were on this back porch, living like rednecks, laughing like little kids, and hopefully when the night was done, screwing like rabbits.

The next summer I lived at the beach again with some more of my best friends in a house that some would call a refugee camp. My dream girl lived a few houses down and was dumb enough to hook up with a shoeless beach bum like me for the summer. We played putt putt in the house on rainy days, went to the beach every other day and lived much of the same life as we did in summer 2012. There was one exception: we had no hot water. All of our budgets were tight and we had to choose between cable or gas and hot water. The NBA Finals were coming up and everyone in the house either hated or loved LeBron, so we took cold showers every day that summer so that we could see the Heat beat the Spurs in seven.

We would rip dollars in half so that we could get two of us onto the bus for the price of one, cramming the halved dollars into the thing faster than anyone could see. Banksy and I even had a joint checking account that summer. By that I mean, we would both put our tips money in a cooler on the top bunk (Banks slept on a mattress on the ground this summer so the top bunk was open). Whenever we needed money, we'd just reach into the cooler and grab a fiver or, if we were lucky a tenner, not really knowing or caring whose it originally was.

Those summers changed my life. They were like a switch in my entire mindset where I went from thinking that I was going to be one of those guys that had to have the big house with the fancy car to thinking that I was going to be the guy that didn't need all that. If it came, I'd be thrilled, sure, but I resolved to place the life part first and then maybe the big house and nice car would work itself out. It's the reason I moved to San Diego in the first place without a job or a place to live. I said I'd do everything to make sure I had as many days like the summers of 2012 and 2013.

That time in my life was my introduction to minimalism and all of its benefits. In *The More of Less: Finding the Life You Want Under Everything You Own*, Joshua Becker talks about these universal benefits and how in a world that is so obsessed with material possessions and having more, we often are blinded by what is the most important. Our houses are getting bigger, yet I was happiest in a beach shack that was the smallest place I ever lived. We are consuming more, whether that is materials or media, yet I was happiest when my beers were cheapest, my clothes were the same everyday, and my drinking games and parties were simplest.

There were two universal benefits that Becker talked about that stood out the most to me. The first was that minimalism caused less distraction. By having more, you are naturally going to want to use more of these things, and can easily end up distracted by what you really want to do and the possessions you actually care about. You have too much, so you focus too little on the things that matter because you don't have enough focus to go around. When I lived in those shacks, I had to focus on waking up, making sure that I had a dry pair of trunks, and that it wasn't raining outside. The beach was my only option really, and it made it an easy choice, because the beach is always the best choice. I had one option of clothes, and I'm never more comfortable than when I have a pair of board shorts on and nothing on my chest except the hot sun cooking me. I was less distracted because I never needed to decide what to do. I had it all laid out in front of me.

The other benefit of minimalism that stuck with me in Becker's book was the idea of doing less comparison. When you play the game of who has most, there will always be a loser. Unless you're Jeff Bezos, you are one of those losers. We constantly compare our lives to others and try to get what they have, trying to have the experiences that they do (Becker, p. 8-11).[6] When I lived at the beach, I didn't have an ounce of jealousy for whatever anyone else was doing. With just the things that I had around me, I had the same thought as Bruce did when he was around that age... I had it all, and looking back now, maybe I did. I didn't wish I was on some cruise that a buddy of mine was on; I was happy that I had a white trash themed party to look forward to that night. I wasn't thinking about the wagyu steak that anyone else was eating; I was just enjoying the fact that I was able to put Lay's potato chips in my PB&J, and it was at ten out of ten every time. I wasn't thinking, "fuck, I wish I had a hot shower today like everyone else." Instead, I was thinking, "it's so hot out today, I'm gonna shower outside using the hose and kill two birds with one stone. It will wash my trunks and me at the same time and it'll be a blast doing it." I was only comparing my own options, and oftentimes those were easy decisions. No matter what, I was coming out a winner.

My ideal life didn't need all the fluff as long as I was doing what I liked to do with the people that meant the most to me, hopefully in a place with some salt. I could be happy with just the beach, a bucket, a cold beer, a cold shower, and my buddies... and of course two plastic knives and some duct tape in case of an emergency. Our pleasures across the board were the simplest and the most abundant compared to any other time in my life. This was the formula that I've carried with me to this point. It was huge underlying reason why I knew I could be happy living in almost any conditions, with the less maybe even being the best, including the back of a pickup truck.

3

PICKUP TRUCK

(1:06)

I had lived in San Diego for two years and by all accounts life was good. I had an amazing group of friends, a solid job, and I lived 5 blocks from the most important thing in the world to me: the ocean. Somehow it just wasn't enough, though. Even though I was happier than I had been in years, I was still lacking in total fulfillment. I was missing something.

Like I said, my job was solid, but I felt like I really had no purpose. Growing up, I always imagined something bigger for myself in life than being a supply planner for a bamboo company. For the most part, I liked the people I worked with, the benefits were good, and the working environment was relaxed. I just had grander ambitions for myself and not achieving those yet freaked me out.

The worst part about my quarter life crisis was my anxiety, which kicked in to full effect due to all of the aforementioned problems and other things that I was dealing with in my own head. To tell you the truth, I didn't even know that I had anxiety. I thought that I was just a worry wart and this was how everybody generally thought, my case just being more extreme. It wasn't until one of my friends came and told me that his girlfriend had it and was going through some shit. I bought him a book on it so he could understand what she was going through and a copy of it for myself so that I could help give him knowledgeable advice whenever he needed it. Like I said, I didn't know what it was; so, if he were to ask me about it, I'd just have to give some half-assed advice on what I was thinking that it was. I didn't have to get my PhD in it, but I wanted to at least be able to understand what she was going through, and in turn, understand what my boy was going through.

The book was called *Monkey Mind* by a guy named Daniel Smith who had anxiety himself, as did his mother. He described his anxious mind very early on in the book with the below passage:

> A typical line of thought went something like this: *I am anxious. The anxiety makes it impossible to concentrate. Because it is impossible to concentrate, I will make an unforgivable mistake at work. Because I will make an unforgivable mistake at work, I will be fired. Because I will be fired, I will not be able to pay my rent. Because I will not be able to pay my rent, I will be forced to have sex for money in an alley behind Fenway Park. Because I will be forced to have sex for money in an alley behind Fenway Park, I will contract HIV. Because I will contract HIV, I will develop full-blown AIDS. Because I will develop full-blown AIDS, I will die disgraced and alone* (Smith, 4).[7]

I instantly connected with the way this guy thought. I could work myself into the same types of fits. The more I read of it, the more I knew that this was exactly what I was going through and I never knew it. There is nothing about me that makes me qualified to talk about the science of anxiety or the psychology behind it for other people. I do not want anyone to self-diagnose based on reading what my experience with my anxiety was. The truth is, it is pretty common with almost three out of ten Americans suffering from it[6], and each case is different from the others. My case is much more mild than most, but it can flare up and get bad at times, and I've had a few panic attacks, luckily not too many. I can only speak of my own experience, of why I knew that what I had read was what I was going through, and how I was going to try to ease it.

I always knew I was a hypochondriac. I would get a tickle in my throat, fire up WebMD and sure enough, there it was: throat cancer, two months to live. Seriously, fuck the guy that writes the WebMD algorithms. True story, one time my college roommate and one of my best friends, Dillon, and I stayed up all night itching and scratching because someone we knew had scabies and we thought for sure that we had it too. We were up until 04:00 scratching ourselves like Woogie from *There's Something About Mary* and when we got to the early morning doctors appointments the next day, they told each of us the same thing: no scabies. My doc, a nice Indian gentleman with an even nicer accent, even went as far as to say "and to prove that you don't have a tha scabies, I shake your hand."

My hypochondria never meant much to me, though. I thought it was just something everyone bugged out about and mine was just way worse than others. It's something I still can laugh about and all of my friends know about. For a while, my biggest fears were pink eye and mono, and as soon as I heard someone had it, I was washing my hands like the Aviator. It wasn't until I read *Monkey Mind* that I learned that hypochondria was a form of anxiety and my anxiety was much deeper than just worrying about my health when I wasn't sick.

As I mentioned earlier, my job was fine and the people were great, but I still wasn't fully engaged there. My issue with the job was the job itself. I liked being a supply planner; it was more interesting to me than most jobs, deciding inventory levels and how much to buy, but I didn't jump out of bed to do it. My aspirations were always to be an entrepreneur, to work for myself. The idea hadn't come to me yet and that would stress me out. I thought if I didn't think of one soon, then I'd work this job the rest of my life looking at a computer buying someone else's bamboo to sit in a warehouse for someone else to sell. It freaked me out and I lost hours of sleep over it, adding up to days over the year probably.

It wasn't that I wanted an out, or didn't want to work hard. Quite the opposite actually, I was one of two outstanding seniors in high school out of a class of 351. I was on the Dean's list every semester in college and busted my ass in all of my life pursuits. I liked working hard, but I just needed to work hard toward something that meant something to me. I lacked purpose, which I found to be one of the most important keys to my happiness. When I was driving hard towards something, whether that was the State Championship in high school or working on a project that did mean something to me at work, the grind to get to that goal was pure bliss to me.

Another one of my keys to happiness was relationships. I had the best friends a guy could ask for. From my boys back home, the Gin Bandits, to the pals I had made on the west coast, I knew I had a loyal group of guy friends that would have my back through and through. My girl friends (two words) weren't half bad either. I had some absolute sweethearts on both coasts that I could always count on if I ever needed a woman's perspective for advice that my guy friends would laugh at me for asking. My girlfriends (one word) were lacking though, and I was lonely.

I tried it all. I downloaded the stupid apps, only to delete them a few weeks later once I saw how many matches my more attractive buddies were getting, compared to how few I was getting. If anything, it was tearing my confidence down making me less confident when talking to real people in real life. Most of the matches I was getting were bots that would immediately hit me with something like, "hey :-) ur really cute. We should meet up and have sex sometime. Meet me in my chat room www.sexwithgirls.com/Imarealperson." I was over it, so I deleted all of the apps.

Everyone always says how great being single is, but my theory is they're just saying that so they can look like it's their choice to make them more attractive to the women they want to be their girlfriends. I never tried that tactic, but as I'm typing this I'm realizing the sheer genius of it. I never said I liked being single. I hate it actually and I had never really experienced it until I was midway through college while everyone else had already developed their "game." I had been single for four years and thought about it constantly. I was constantly looking for my next girlfriend even if I knew she wasn't the right one.

Here is a perfect example of my spiraling anxiety: every single time I failed with a girl, no matter the girl, the outcome of that failure was that I was never going to get married. I had a girlfriend in middle school that once wrote me, "Your biggest fear is clogging someone else's toilet. Mine is losing you." Talk about simpler times. My biggest fear now was dying alone. Though not as extreme or graphic as Daniel Smith's, I could work my way into the same unwinding towards a similar ending with a thought process like this:

"This girl doesn't like me. She doesn't like me because of (insert any and every negative thought that I have about myself). Every girl probably thinks this. That's why it didn't work out with her, and the last one, and the one before that, and the one before that... I'm already 25, I thought I'd be married by now. My biological clock is TICKIN! What if I don't find a girl by 30, every good girl out there will be snatched up by then. I'm never getting married. I'm going to die alone."

All of this snowball because Maria from the bar didn't respond to my text when I thought we had hit it off, or Rosie from Bumble didn't send a message even though we "matched." It sounds dramatic, and I was, no doubt. This, however, was exactly how my mind worked and I couldn't shake it. People would tell me it's no big deal and they were probably right, but in my head, it was a huge, compounding deal, with each failure or rejection adding to the last and being the worst of all. I saw a therapist for a little while, and that helped in a monumental way, but the longer I spent away from it, the worse my anxiety would build.

So between the fear of loneliness paired with the perfect girl I knew was out there, and the job I didn't love paired with the dream job I envisioned for myself, and a million other little things that I won't get into, I had a ton of anxiety building up that made me hate being alone. The smallest everyday situations could send my mind into a tailspin where I could get from a small worry to the thought that my entire life is heading in the wrong direction. My mind had a motor that wouldn't quit and it ran all day everyday. Here comes the worst part: because of this anxiety, I spent most of my time alone. My thought process was just go home and relax on the couch, watch some TV, or surf the mindless internet and forget about the other stuff. This was a band aid for my mind. Endorphins weren't being released; I was just numbing myself to everything, walking on autopilot. I'm not alone in this cycle. A study from my alma mater, the University of Maryland, describes how people that spent more time watching television were generally less happy. They also found that watching television was rewarding in the short term, but over time made people feel more uneasy (Robinson & Martin).[8] I would get into the house and do all that mindless shit until it was time to go to bed when all of the other stuff would catch up to me and I'd lay awake for hours running through regrets in past lives and worrying about how I could add more in the future.

I wasn't doing enough of the stuff I was passionate about like surfing, bike riding, exercising, spending time with friends, all because I thought I was giving my mind a break. In reality I was building my mind a dam for my problems and a flood was inevitable. Some days, I'd go to work from 08:00 to 16:30, get home at 17:00, watch TV until 21:00 with dinner somewhere in between and then go lie in bed for an hour or two in a mono y mono duke fest of PFG versus his monkey mind. Don't get me wrong, this wasn't every day. I still did surf and did all that other stuff I loved before I moved into the truck, but I had too many days of the other routine that I knew it was time for a change.

In *Monkey Mind* it talks about some of the techniques of coping with anxiety. One is called flooding, and it basically entails taking whatever your worst fear or worry is, and attacking it head on.[7] See what your fear is and why you are afraid of it, and realize that it is not as bad as you are thinking. Once you're able to see that, you'll worry about it less. No, I did not quit my job to tackle my fear of lacking a purpose. No, I did not lick the floor of a subway station to overcome my hypochondria. I needed to flood the root of all of the problems, my fear of my own mind and spending time with it.

So I made the most extreme change that I could think of. I was going to move into a camper shell in the back of my truck. I'd flood myself with the fear of being alone, by living alone and forcing myself to be alone most of the day. I couldn't watch an episode of Entourage to kill the time before bed, or spend time just laying in bed feeling sorry for myself. I was going to be living in a little box and I would have to go out and live it. Even on days I wanted to sulk, I'd have to face the big, beautiful world and say, "here I am, come and get me." I'd have nowhere else to turn, to turtle up and hide when things got tough. I wouldn't have roommates to shoot the shit with, I'd just have myself and I'd have to learn to like being with that person.

This wasn't just some rash decision or something I thought up to punish myself. I thought back to the times that I was the happiest, living in Ocean City, and realized the minimalist, beach bum lifestyle could probably do me some good. Dillon and I always dreamed about building a bus or a tiny house that we could live on and travel the country, but it never seemed feasible. We were obsessed with the idea, me specifically, talking for hours about how we'd outfit it, where we'd go, what we'd do with all the money we saved, the whole nine. It was a dream of mine; I just never had the stones to do it, or the drive to start it.

Dillon was living in Jacksonville now and I was 3000 miles away, so building a bus or tiny house alone would have probably set me back 10-30 boxes of ziti. And I didn't have the spare boxes of ziti to do that. What was the next best thing? A van, but I didn't have one of those and that'd be another couple grand and another set of car insurance, etc. What was the next best thing after that? A camper shell on my truck.

I had the truck, all I needed was a camper shell, which was about a month's worth of rent. So I figured I could swing it; if I made it one month of living in there and then moved out, then no harm no foul. I wouldn't lose any money, if anything I'd just add value to my truck. Worst case, I could sell it for a small loss because these things kept their value. There was not really any financial risk. I knew that if I really hated it, I could live on a buddy's couch for a bit while I found my own place, so there was not really much risk there. It sounded pretty feasible.

I started doing some research on how other people built theirs out. I'd Google, "truck shell conversions" or check Pinterest to get inspiration on what everyone had already made. Most people did it strictly for camping, but there were some pretty sweet setups. I saw some with two beds, each with drawers underneath, and a middle section that was empty for moving around. I saw some with beds low to the bed of the truck and a hammock looking thing on the top for their storage. I decided on a set up of a full bed with drawers of storage underneath. I'd spend downtime at work drawing up the plans, with measurements and what pieces of wood I would need. I made lists of the things that I would keep in the drawers, where I would keep them, trying to trim down the list to as small as possible. I started to get pretty stoked about it.

Then came the harsh reality; I had to tell people that I was doing this. The first person I told was Dillon. I knew he'd be all for it, if anything telling me I *wouldn't* follow through with it, using it as his way to motivate me more. My next buddy to tell was Kenny. He had been traveling for the past few months since his contract as a financial analyst for a bank had ran out.

He actually lived out of his SUV for 30 days in a cross country road trip and survived it, so I knew it was something I could do. He was the most positive, energetic person I knew, so I knew I could count on him to support my decision too. He did; in fact, he was thrilled with it.

I told the people that were jacked up about it and told them not to tell people as I wanted to explain it to them myself (a sentiment I still feel about the experience). They were the easy people to tell. It would only get harder as I knew I had to tell people that may or may not understand. I called each of my other closest friends, the Gin Bandits, and explained what I was doing. I knew that even if they didn't understand, they'd support me and that's pretty much exactly how it went.

I called Brendan, my oldest friend, and explained the what and why. I went up to my balcony and hit the Favorite on my iPhone, shaking with nerves. He worked as a Financial Planner and wore a suit everyday, was sharp as a tack, had the beautiful girlfriend, and by all means the All American life. Brendan is the last type of person that I could expect doing something like this, so I knew that if he understood and supported me, I could go through with it. When I got done explaining it, I could tell he was smiling on the other end of the phone. I was nervous about what he'd say, but I never should have been. He said, "I always had a feeling you'd do something like this. Don't get me wrong, I'd never do it, but if you think you'll be alright, I'm pumped for you. I just want you to be happy, man." He always said that last sentence to me, and he really meant it. I knew that this was a wild way to try to seek that happiness, but hell, I had to try it.

Lastly, I told the people that I knew would not understand. I tried to hold off as long as possible, but it all came to a head one day when we were talking about future living situations. I had kept my ideas mostly to myself around my friends in San Diego because our group of friends busted a lot of balls. Since I was feeling a little shaky about the idea, the last thing I wanted was for people to shit on me until they talked me out of it.

Everyone kept asking where I was going to live because they knew our lease was running up and I was the only one of my roommates without a confirmed plan. I'd say that I was going to find a place of my own so that I could rent it out and travel on the weekends. It was about two weeks out and I hadn't been spending a lot of time on my computer looking for a place, and never went on an open house visit or anything, so people were starting to get curious.

Then, one day, my buddy MC had just about had enough and said, "Dude, why the fuck are you being so sketchy about it? Where are you living?"

"I'm not sure yet..." I sheepishly replied.

"What are you gonna do? Live in your fucking pickup truck?!" he said with a chuckle as if there was no way that was the answer. A while back, I had told him about my plan to travel in the truck and Airbnb my place on the weekends, which was a plan that I really had considered. So he knew that was an option, but I'm telling you he was not prepared for my response.

"Yes. You know what, that's exactly what I'm doing," I defensively kind of snapped at him.

"Get the fuck out of here," he said with a condescending laugh, "you're telling me you're gonna live out of your fucking truck..." he continued, giving me a confused look that I can still vividly picture.

I was short about it but explained that this was what I wanted to do. He just couldn't understand it, so after a bit I changed the subject, hung around for a little, and then went up to my room to let the rest of them hang out... and probably shit talk me while they digested it and I wasn't in the room. I hung out on my balcony, questioning myself, fuming about my friend cutting me up.

What bothered me most wasn't that he didn't understand it, it was the fact that he didn't care to understand it. To him it was just a stupid fucking idea that he would never do, so nobody should do it. I had some people tell me they would love to do it and others tell me "I'd never do that, but that's awesome that you're trying it," which I always appreciated. But here was one of my best friends making me feel two inches tall for going for it. I had expected this kind of response from people, but not from a close friend. He was really the only one that ever gave me that type of response. That's probably because most people that I wasn't as close with wanted to be polite. He could give it to me straight since our bond was so strong, but it still bugged me.

Once everyone knew, there was no turning back. I was telling other people my goals to have them hold me accountable and make sure I actually followed through. Now all there was to do was build my new home.

4

SHELTER FROM THE STORM

(2:15)

Once it was real, and there was no way but forward, my work drawing sessions got more serious. I began thinking of every little detail. I would plan out my hypothetical days and think of how everything I did in a "normal" life living in an apartment could all be compressed into this truckin' thang. I would draw up a page, rip it up, draw something entirely different on a post-it and stare at it for a few days before crumpling it and tossing it out. I must have gone through a whole pad of post its of my little drawings, and I may be the least artistic person I know, so they weren't pretty.

The measurements I got from the actual truck bed, the size of the wood I was planning to use, and the expected height that I would need were all taken into account. I bought the shell from a LEER dealership and took the measurements from top to bottom. I got one of the shells that was the same height as the height of the truck so that it looked as inconspicuous as possible. I decided the height of the bed frame was going to need to be no more than 15 inches so that I could have enough space to be comfortable between the roof and my body when I was laying down. I probably could have squeezed a few more inches, but that would have risked a lot more of me banging my head on the roof when I'd wake up. It was a risk that I simply was not willing to take.

The width of the drawers was easy. There would need to be a small piece of plywood at the bottom to fit in between the wheel wells, then large planks standing up vertically on top of that bottom piece. In between these vertical pieces would be the slots that the drawers would slide into. On top of the vertical planks would be eight 2x4s to keep it sturdy and then another, larger piece of plywood on top of that. I finally got the blueprint I liked and was ready to take it to my wood guy to get the cuts I needed. By that, I mean I went to Home Depot and had them make the exact cuts I needed on the wood to build out the entire frame and the shelves.

Wood, check. Next thing I had to get was screws and wood glue. I grabbed the silver screws that looked long enough to go from the 2x4s into the plywood and keep them steady. My buddy, Chof, was going to let me borrow his drill, so all I needed to do was make sure I picked a screw size that was compatible with one of the drill bits that I had. How could I mess this up?

It was going to be a pretty simple structure, made up of just wood, glue and screws. I didn't feel like my shelves needed the crazy wheeling mechanisms to slide in and out. I didn't need any secret hatches for me to hide my contraband. I just needed something to store my clothes and support my body weight when I went to sleep.

My construction site would be the balcony off of my room in my apartment. I moved all of the furniture to the edges of the balcony and placed all my materials in the middle. Since it never rained in San Diego, I wasn't worried about it raining on my future furniture, but I was worried about the fat seagull that always hung around there literally shitting on it. There was enough space out there to maneuver, but it would be a little tight. It was the only workshop I had, though; so, it would have to do.

The first step would be to build the outer structure of the bedframe. I'd need to glue the three massive wooden planks vertically on the smaller piece of plywood and let that dry for a few hours. Once it was dry, I glued the 2x4s horizontally across them and let that dry for another day. Then, I drilled the pilot holes into the 2x4s and through the planks to get them ready for the screws. It was all smooth sailing until the next step where I had to drill in the screws. This was where my stubbornness and lack of knowledge in the field of carpentry was absolutely exposed. The first one or two were difficult, but eventually went through and were close enough to being flush with the boards. After those, it was two bad screws to each one properly screwed in one. In other words, I would screw it in about half way and then it would get stuck. No matter how hard I tried, these things would not budge.

If I would have just let the first few half screwed in ones be the only ones, figured out why it was happening and then fixed the problem, I would have saved myself a lot of time and frustration. Why would I do that though? That would make too much sense. Instead, I thought to myself, "That was just a bad screw, the next one will go in." And so it went. I screwed in probably thirty screws with ten being in all the way, ten being three quarters in, and ten being half way in with a big screw hanging out that would neither go in any further, nor come out completely. I tried Googling how to get them down or even out, but nothing. One thing said to put a rubber band over the screw and then use the drill to loosen it up. I tried this rubber band trick, but that just led to a fucked up rubber band and a more frustrated PFG.

MC came over to help out. Even though he hadn't understood the truck move and didn't agree with it, he was still a hell of a friend and was there to help me out. He had worked a few summers for his uncle's carpentry company so he knew his way around a drill a little bit and he was a meatstick of muscle. He was able to get a couple of them in by putting more force into the drill and getting a little more weight behind it using some techniques his uncle had showed him, but there were still a lot of screws that were a shitshow. Muscle man MC couldn't get the rest of 'em in and the rubber band trick couldn't get 'em out, so I had this hunk of wood with screws in it that I couldn't lay the last piece of plywood on and definitely couldn't just leave as is.

It was time to enlist the help of someone else. I called Brendan, who used to work for our friend's dad, Mr. Steve or "Chief" as we called him. Chief owned his own construction business and knew everything about building anything. He had shown Brendan the ropes over those summers, so I was hoping he'd have an answer.

"Well are you Sallying it?" Brendan asked, inferring that these screws were not going in just because I was being a big pansy and not putting enough force behind it. I told him that I wished that were the case, but these things were just stuck like King Arthur's sword… or in this case swords, a lot of swords. He chuckled and said, "Well why didn't you just stop after a couple?!" We laughed about it for a little because I wished I had the answer to that one too, but I didn't. Stupid pride, I guess, that was the only answer that there was.

Finally, after Brendan made me feel worse than before I called for help, I had to call in the big guns: Chief. I hadn't spoken to him in a couple years, since I had driven across the country to move to California asking him recommendations for places to eat. Chief was the biggest foodie I knew and he used to take all of our friends and a few of the dads on road trips just to get famous food places. He was one of the funniest people I had ever met and was always willing to help out us kids, so I knew he'd be eager to help me out and like I said, he knew his shit so he would be able to give me sound guidance.

I went to a local hardware store this time to get my new materials. It was Home Depot's fault after all, since they gave me the faulty screws! I had to try a place with real screws. I knew it was actually the wizard's fault not the wand, meaning me and not the screws. However, if I was calling Chief, I wanted to call him from a local shop. He used to often say, "you always support the local guy." So if I called from Home Depot or Lowe's, the call would have started off on the wrong foot.

I tried him and he didn't pick up the first time, like always. I remember growing up, people would call him and he'd fumble around with his ear piece in the car, finally getting it into his ear. "This is Steve," he'd finally say when the damn thing worked, only to hear nothing on the other end because he took too long to get on the horn. I knew he'd call me back and he did.

"F'er!" he said when I picked up. He always called me PFer, as long as I could remember. We hadn't spoken in a few years, but with how easy he was to talk to and with our longtime bond, you would have thought we had spoken earlier this morning.

I lied and told him I was building a dresser because I hadn't even told my folks about my new truck life experiment. I figured it would be pretty rude for them to hear it from my buddy's dad rather than from me. I told him the gist of my problem with the screws and asked if he knew why it was happening and how I could get it out.

"What color screws are they?" he asked.

"Silver, why?" I replied confused as hell. I couldn't understand why the color would matter. I figured silver, stainless steel screws would be the best thing for the job. Silver had to be the right answer to his question, he probably just wanted to make sure.

"Ugh. Were they shiny?" he asked me, almost in disgust.

"Yeah, they were shiny." Isn't shiny a good thing? People love bright, shiny things. Shouldn't nice screws be shiny? At this point I was wondering if he was fucking with me.

"Ah dammit PF'er. You've gotta get the black screws. The shiny silver ones are junk, for chumps. Get the black ones and they'll slide in like prom night." He explained that with the wood that I was using, I would need "Fine Drywall Screws." I guess those only ever came in black, never ever silver.

I can honestly say I will never, ever, buy silver screws again. You'd more likely find me hitting an orange ball on the golf course than using silver screws again. I felt like the biggest hack of a carpenter, and was embarrassed that I even had to tell him with how disgusted he was in my shiny, pretty boy screws. Building things with your hands isn't about being flashy. Why would I have ever gotten shiny screws when the solid, practical, black screws were right next to them?

"Okay, I'll do that. What about the half screws that are in there already? How do I get them out?" I asked.

He ran through all of the tricks that I had Googled that didn't work and then finally I told him that I was putting a board, the plywood that would lie on top of the 2x4s, over these screws so they needed to be flush down.

"Oh, these screws aren't gonna be seen? F'er, why didn't you say so? Just take a hacksaw to 'em and shave 'em down to make them level with the board. If you can't see 'em who cares how you get them down." I didn't think a saw could do that to metal, and he reminded me that was the exact kind of use for a hacksaw.

I asked for any last pieces of advice and he said, "When you drill the new pilot holes for the fine black drywall screws, drop a little drop a dishsoap in there and the screws will go in like an out-of-town date." In case you couldn't tell, Steve loved the out of town date or prom night lines and it was the hundredth time I had heard each, but neither got old.

I left the hardware store with a hacksaw and my new *black* screws, feeling confident that I'd be able to get this project back on the right track. When I got home, I went straight to the workshop with my new saw. It was about 90 degrees up there on that balcony in the San Diego Indian Summer heat, but I was determined to get these things shaved down. I took to the first one and the sound that this saw made against my silver screws was worse than nails on a chalkboard and cardboard scraping against cardboard combined. The good news though: it worked. The screw was off, only nineteen more to go. I stayed up there for a couple hours, hacking away with this awful noise and probably pissing my soon to be former neighbors off to no end. At least it was in the middle of the day, but I can't imagine that the horrendous sound was well received. Soaking in sweat, with metal sawdust all over my hands and a few cuts from scraping my knuckles against the wood while sawing, I stood up there exhausted, but victorious. Time to get back to work

Chief didn't disappoint. Armed with new screws, dish soap, and some new techniques MC had shown me to get behind the drill to get the force to drill them down, the screws slid right in. He wasn't lying; I had gone from King Arthur's sword for screws to out-of-town date screws, sliding right in. I also flipped the frame over and drilled the plywood into the vertical planks so that they were fully secure.

When I flipped it back over, I sat on some of the 2x4s to see how she would hold. When I put my full weight on it and could feel no budge or movement at all, I stood up and looked at the base of what would be my bed someday and felt mighty proud. I hadn't felt this way since I replaced my car's side view mirror. I felt like a real man. Ask any man if they can tell you a better feeling than fixing something with their own two hands; I bet they can't.

Next, I glued the larger piece of plywood over top of the 2x4s. The plywood is there so that when the mattress pad goes on top, it is flat. If it was just the pad over the 2x4s, the pad would have squiggled in out of the gaps between them. That would be a sure way to permanently ruin my back. After that, I drilled pilot holes (with dishsoap obviously) and drilled some black screws into the top plywood piece that sat on the 2x4s.

It really looked like a bed frame now. I was just going to have to build some drawers to slide into the slots between the vertical planks holding the 2x4s up. I took the measurements on what would need to fill the empty slots and headed back to Home Depot to get my cuts and my little knobs that I'd use to pull the drawers out. I got some classy gold knobs with a swirly design. I began to think that this was going to be the nicest looking homeless truck bed the world ever seen.

The drawers would be long as they went as deep as the length of the truck bed. I'd make partitions in the drawers to separate the different sets of clothes to keep everything organized. The partitions were spaced apart equidistant from each other and perpendicular to the long side walls of the drawers. If you stood them up straight, the drawers would essentially look like book cases.

I decided that the left drawer would have most of my clean clothes. When I pulled out the drawer, the first section would be socks and underoos on one side, divided by a thin piece of plywood and my trunks and gym shorts on the other side. This would be the only section of a drawer that was divided in the middle, perpendicular to all of the other drawer partitions. Neither of those things needed a full section, but both needed to be easily accessible. The next section would be my pants, followed by a section for shirts that I could wear to work, and then a section for my sweatshirts, jackets, etc. Since I needed these the least often in San Diego, it made sense for them to be furthest back.

Fortunately, I worked for a laid back enough company that I didn't need to wear nice clothes all the time. I could leave my suits, dress shirts, and slacks in my storage unit. I definitely had to up my folding game when I moved into the truck though so that all of my business casual clothes — the short sleeve button downs, polos, and "nice" t-shirts — were neat enough to not be wrinkled like I just pulled them out of a drawer in my truck.

The drawer on the right side would be dirty clothes, gym clothes, and anything else I needed to throw back there. This was essentially the junk drawer. The first section, which was about 2.5 times the size of a normal section in the left drawer would be my "hamper." It was going to hold all of the dirty clothes and needed to be the first section so that I could easily pull out and throw my dirties in there. My laundry detergent and dryer sheets were also stored at the bottom of this drawer so that whenever I had to do laundry, there they were for me while I was grabbing all of the dirties. The next section would be my workout shirts or just shirts that I wore to be comfortable. The last section would be for random shit like an extra blanket or one off clothes that I needed more than just once a month like pajamas or sweatpants.

I measured the cuts of plywood for the bottoms of the drawers so that they would have about an eighth of an inch on each side. This way they wouldn't be banging around on the sides, but would also slide in, like my friend Chief says, "like prom night." The face of the drawers, where the knobs would be, would stick out a little further on each side so that they stopped right where the frame began when they were pushed in. Once the frames of the drawers were glued and dried, I drilled them together and slid them in. All it needed now was a fresh paint job.

I prepped the wood for the paint first by sanding the whole thing down. Since the bottom of the bedframe would never be seen, I left it alone and just painted the top and sides. The drawers were painted completely. The paint I used was Red Walnut and it looked like something that would have belonged in the home of George Washington. It was rustic looking, but with class. Lastly, I screwed in the knobs, two for each drawer face, equidistant from each other and lined up horizontally.

Goddamn it, I was proud of it. When the paint dried, I decided to lay down on it and picture myself sleeping on it for a few months. The top surface of the bedframe was only 52 by 60, which means it was not long enough to sleep straight, even for a shorter gentleman like myself. I was going to have to sleep diagonally, but I knew that all along. In fact, when I was doing my architectural drawing sessions on post-it notes, I actually used the Pythagorean theorem to see how much space I would have diagonally. Who would have ever thought I'd ever have to use that shit for something useful? There was enough space for me to get my whole body on it and it didn't wiggle an inch. It was as hard as the pavement that it would soon be parked on, so I couldn't imagine a lot of sleep happening without the mattress pad on yet. But it was sturdy and I had built it, so it felt like a bed fit for a king.

I enlisted my friend, Sock, to help me take the thing down from my workshop, the balcony, to my truck in the garage. Thank god there was an elevator, because getting it there was a process. My sturdy bed frame was as heavy as a ton of bricks. Was Sock thrilled to be hauling it? No, but I really appreciated it and when I saw it fit so snugly into my truck bed, I was beaming.

"Dude, you're gonna be claustrophobic as fuck," Sock said, basically shocked that I was really going through with it now that he had seen my vision come to life.

This was a fact that I was well aware of before I built it, but honestly I had a little more room than I had expected and this was what I was signing up for. I knew that I would not want to be hanging out in there playing my guitar or watching Netflix, so all I had to ask was, "was this enough for me to be okay to get in and out of and sleep comfortably?" To me, the answer was a resounding yes.

The day came when I was ready to move all of my stuff in. I put my cooler and a little storage cabinet with little things I thought I needed in the cab of my truck and then moved all of my clothes and shoes in. The shoes would go in the section where the wheel wells were, between the edges of the drawers and the side of the truck bed and underneath the top of the bed frame that extended over top of the wheel wells.

I put the tapestry I had in my room to hang over top of me and block out the side windows so that nobody could see in, and hung black curtains over the back window where I would come in from. I used Velcro to keep these things up, which was an idiotic mistake, but it got the job done for the first couple of nights. It was a purple tapestry with a sun and waves and it could not have made me look more like a hippy. It might as well have said, "I live inside of this thing," but I have to say I loved how it looked in there. It made it feel more homey. It was a tapestry that just took up a piece of a wall in my room when I lived in an apartment, but now it would take up every inch of my walls and ceilings.

After the decor was hung, I hauled down the memory foam mattress pad that I bought on Amazon. I had cut it down to fit into the truck bed using an X-acto knife and it fit like a glove on top of the bedframe. I added the sheets and blanket, threw my pillows in and it looked like a pretty cozy little place to rest my head.

The last thing that I needed to do was build my "locks." I had originally thought that you would be able to lock the truck shell from the inside. I could lock the tailgate so that nobody could get into the drawers, but I didn't have a way to lock the hatch door so that nobody could get to the other precious cargo: me. You could lock the hatch from the outside with a key, but it was impossible to lock from the inside. I figured out that when you locked it from the outside, there were two metal bars, one on each side, that went from pointing straight up to pointing straight out. These bars extended from the hatch over into the shell when they pointed out (locked) so that when you tried to pull it from the outside, the metal bars stopped the hatch from coming open. I could push these bars down to point out, but if they weren't locked from the outside, then someone could turn the knobs from the outside up and hop right in to snuggle with PFG.

My truck had tie down anchors that were attached to the truck bed and were between the drawers and the sides of the truck bed, so they were accessible. I decided to get some metal wire and attach one end of the wire to the tie down anchor attached to the truck. Then, I'd coil the other end of the wire into a loop and put the loop through the metal bars that kept the hatch door closed when they pointed outwards. Since these wires were tied down to the truck, they weren't going anywhere, and they were made the perfect length so that I could easily put the loop onto the bar, but when I tried to move the bar up, it got caught and stayed shut. I tried it a few times with the tailgate down from the outside and it held. My security system wasn't going to keep out Danny Ocean, but it would keep out someone that wasn't going to put a ton of effort into getting in and would at the very least wake me up if someone was trying to get in.

As Dillon put it, "Dude, if someone wants to get in, they're gonna get in." I'm not sure that was the most reassuring point to be made, but he was right. If I had some sort of lock, that was sufficient because if someone really did want to break in, then they would just break the window, same as living in a house.

I had a bed, I had a lock, I had a dresser for my clothes, I had some classy decoration in my tapestry. What more did I need? It wasn't exactly the easiest thing to build with my novice carpentry skills, but it was architectural gold in my eyes. It looked exactly like I had pictured it, and I built it all myself. I had built the first home that I would ever own and was ready to come home and hit the hay for night one.

5

MAYBE I'M AMAZED

(0:44)

That first night was a wide range of emotions. This thing I had been thinking of, imagining, and wanting to try for years was finally here. This was the night. My friends were asking if I was nervous for night one. It was a valid question, but I figured that even though it would take a little adjusting, it would be easy early on. I never thought that night one would be a big issue because it would be just like camping for a night. If anything, I would enjoy it early on and then later on be thinking, "wait a second, why am I actually living my life like the world is my campsite?" If I hated it, I could just tough it out for a few days and then find an apartment on Craigslist or something. I didn't want to think that way though. I wanted to think that at the very least, I would make it one month. One month would make the cost of the shell and the building materials a wash with rent.

Night one's parking spot was a side street behind my old apartment. I chose this spot for a few different reasons. It was the easiest place to move all of my stuff from my apartment into my new dwellings. I also wanted to be at a place close to a bathroom in case I needed to pee in the middle of the night. This spot was about a one minute walk from a public restroom by the bay, so that checked that box. I never wanted to park on a street that would get a lot of traffic from people leaving town. My town was a drinking town for sure and one of my roommates had his car hit in the middle of the night by a drunk driver. I knew that I wanted to be away from a main road so that I would be safe from my legs getting squished. Lastly, I knew most of the people in these surrounding houses, so if anyone saw me hopping into the truck, they probably wouldn't think too much of it for one night. Perfect spot, I thought.

It was a Saturday night, but none of my friends were really going out, so I hung at the apartment with the soon-to-be former roommates until about 21:00. I was on the lease until midnight, after all. Then, when I started to feel a little tired and knew it was time, I made the trek down the street, to my new place in the neighborhood.

It was dark outside when I went to get into my shell. The street had a few street lights lining the sidewalks and a few balconies overlooking the area that I would be sleeping in. There were apartments lining both sides of the street. This was good and bad. If an emergency happened, like a San Diego Snuggler trying to find a warm body or a burglar in the market for a new cooler breaking into my truck, then there would be people around to hear it and help if needed.

People and well lit areas also made me nervous, though. It was never my intention to make anyone uncomfortable or make them feel like their neighborhood was unsafe. I wanted to be able to hop back in there without anybody seeing me. If nobody saw the jump, nobody would have any idea that I was in there later on. It just looked like a regular truck parking on a public street. I never wanted a nice, neighboring Nancy to see me climbing back in there and say to her husband, "Oh fuck, some guy just snuck into his camper shell and is living there. He had long hair and a beard too! He's probably a serial killer, Jim. Call the cops, now!"

So when I got to my truck shell, I was very careful to look around. A man in his fifties, gray haired with glasses, was outside smoking a cigarette. This is exactly what I didn't want to happen. As I got closer, I noticed it was a guy that had helped me replace my sideview mirror on my truck. He was a funny old dude that said "wham-o" a bunch, so I figured he'd be fine even if he did see me make the bed jump. Regardless, I waited him out in my truck as I took out my contacts and brushed my teeth. When he finally went inside, I headed around to the back of my rig.

I took out the first of the little keys that the LEER dealership gave me for the shell and unlocked the hatch door handles. Then, I was on to the second little key. This one unlocked the tailgate, so I unlocked that and pulled the tailgate down. I got up and onto the bed, as in the mattress of my new home, not just the bed of my truck, with my feet resting on the dropped tailgate. I took off my shoes and put them in the little side slot where the shoes were to go. As I was doing all of this, I knocked into the back curtains and they fell down. All this time, I was already flustered, looking around, again trying to be on the lookout for neighboring Nancy. "Fuck," I thought, "I'll have to be quick to pick up that curtain as soon as I shut everything so that I can get it back up and stay unseen."

I took my shoes off, then I'd get the rest of my clothes off once I was all set on the inside. I had been a sleep-in-the-nude guy for years, but I figured it was best to sleep in just underoos in this setting. If I were to be exposed by the cops and they saw me sleeping in there, it would probably be a little slap on the wrist. If they saw me sleeping in there and the blankets had fallen off and I was just lying there with my little pepper hanging out, it would be a much tougher conversation. Needless to say, my sleeping in the raw days were put on hold.

I grabbed the tailgate with an awkward, but well-balanced (if I do say so myself), leaning plank out the back and pulled it closed to a loud DOOF. I reached my arm out with the little tailgate key and locked it. I grabbed the metal locking rods of the shell hatch and pulled that down next. Once it was pulled down, I flipped the rods down to be pointing outwards and grabbed my metal wire locking mechanism loops and looped them around the rods. Flustered and sweating a little bit, I reached around for the fallen curtain that covers the hatch door. I put it back up with the velcro, trying not to knock the tapestry down in the process.

I was in. Before I started to get into just my underoos, I peered out the side of the curtain, careful not to knock that down, either. Anxiously, I was scanning the whole street to see if anyone saw me get in and was walking over to the truck to give me a talking to or peering down from their balcony with a telephone in hand, calling John Law. It looked like the coast was clear; I could begin the undressing process.

I took my shirt off first. Trying not to bang my head on the roof, or worse, knock down the tapestry, I hunched down a little bit half sitting up and half laying down. On first attempt, I hit the tapestry with my right arm as I was attempting to lift the shirt off my head. The tapestry fell a little bit and I had to push it back up so that there was not a big hanging thing two inches from my face all night. I wiggled the shirt off and it was on to the shorts. I was lying on my back, so I lifted up my pelvis with both shoulder blades and both feet still planted to the floor and wiggled the shorts off. This was the exact kind of motion that a young man dreams about — when a woman is taking off her underwear in bed, scooting them off with the majority of her body still glued to the bed and then wiggling them off her feet. I can promise you that it was not as attractive when I did it, sweating like a donkey, alone in my truck. Regardless, knowing the motion, I was able to do it pretty smoothly. After all, nothing was knocked down this time.

I wiggled into my position that I had been planning for months. I would sleep diagonally because the shell wasn't long enough for me to sleep straight up and down. In other words, my pillow was on the right side, closer to the front of the truck, and my feet were on the left side of the truck, at the back of the bed. In this positioning, I was able to sprawl out, just like I did in my normal bed. I would lie on my stomach, right ear on the pillow, right leg straight to the back of the bed, left leg in an L shape, right arm under the pillow. Despite the small area, it was pretty comfortable and not far off from a regular bed. I cracked the window open that was closest to my head. This window connected the truck bed to the truck, but also was to the open air of outside. Maybe this was going to be easier than I thought.

So there I was, in my new home. This twenty five year old in his American Eagle boxer shorts, lying on a memory foam mattress pad, in the camper shell on the back of his pickup truck, on a side street behind his old $3000 a month apartment, was ready for his first night of sleep in his new home. It wasn't pretty that first night getting in or getting undressed, but I was ready, or so I thought.

As long as I can remember, I've never been a strong sleeper. It all started when my babysitter gave me the worst advice ever given in the history of mankind. When five year old PFG couldn't sleep one night, he asked her what to do, she said to "just think of things." That was all I ever did from that day on when trying to sleep. I would think and think and think. I'd stay up hours on end just thinking, mostly worrying. So on my first night in the truck, every thought of worry that I had stored up was ready to come out.

I thought about all of the normal things that would keep me up at night when I lived in a house. On top of that I was worrying about the truck things. It would get a little bit hot and I would worry that I was going to get overheated or die from a lack of oxygen, so I opened all of the side windows that were behind the tapestry and ripped off the covers so that I was just laying on top of the sheets. I'd worry about someone breaking in or a car crashing into me speeding down the street. If a car hit me from behind, there was a decent chance it would break my legs. At times it would just hit me, "damn, I am really living in my truck right now. This is the only home I've got." and I would be shook for a second.

The worst thoughts though, were when I would worry about someone walking by and seeing me in there. I had never really had trouble with the law and had always been pretty afraid of the boys in blue even when I wasn't doing anything wrong. What I was doing was illegal, so if someone saw me, they could report me to the police and I could get a ticket or warning. Imagine that: if night one I got my warning. Then I'd have to risk it and keep the truck life going knowing that if I got caught again, there was a chance I'd go to jail. It was either that, or I'd give it up after one night and have it be a total waste of time, money, and energy, not to mention that I would look like the biggest clown to anyone that knew that I was doing it in the first place.

A person would walk by and I would hear their footsteps through the window closest to my head. It felt like their footsteps were matching my heartbeat, as it pounded through my bare chest so hard that I could hear it. I was terrified they'd know that I was in there. How could they? They couldn't see in, but could they hear me breathing or hear that aforementioned pounding heartbeat? They were probably just walking to their apartment on the street, as they were entitled to do, and didn't give a second thought to any of the vehicles that they passed along their way, mine included. The way my mind works though, I was a nuisance to everyone that lived on that block, they knew I was in there, and they were going to call the cops on me.

I would sleep in about twenty minute bursts, but only a few of those. They were long enough to know that I had fallen asleep based on how long it had been since I checked the clock on my phone. They were short enough, though, to not have a dream. After the first three hours of no sleep, which wasn't too unusual for me on a night that I had a lot on my mind, I probably slept twenty minutes for every two hours. In total that got me to about an hour of sleep, if that.

At about five in the morning, I had to go pee, and figured some fresh air and walking around could do me some good. It could tire me out and by the time I got back to the bed, I would be able to just pass right out for a few hours and feel decent by the time I was ready to get up in the morning. I peered out the back window to see if by some off chance, someone was either still up from the night out, or up early walking the dog or something. The coast looked to be clear, so I flipped the metal loops off of the locks, pushed the hatch open, unlocked the tailgate, dropped it down, stood on the tailgate and then hopped onto the street.

It was that part of the morning where the dawn was just starting to break, so it was still dark, but you could tell that it was going to be light soon. The streetlights had been turned off by then, so the little light from the moon and the nearing sunrise were all that illuminated the path from my bedroom to the bathroom (my truck to the public restroom). The streets were finally quiet and nobody was around, so it was actually a pretty peaceful stroll to the pisser.

I got to the public restroom and it was one of those restrooms where each toilet had its own door to the outside and then there was one big sink area out in the middle. I felt like these were nicer than the restrooms with one door into the whole place and then urinals and stalls lining the walls. It was like the classy motel of public restrooms. I got to the first door there and the light was on, so I moved on to the next one, figuring someone was in the first one. The next one had no light on and was unlocked. It was five in the morning, so I figured if anyone else happened to be up and taking a piss at the public restroom, they'd at least have the light on.

I didn't knock and I walked in. As I pushed open the door, swinging from right to left, I first saw the toilet and then as I pushed the door open further, I saw a man sitting on the concrete corner bench all the way to the left in the stall. It was only a brief split second of seeing this man before I closed the door in a complete panic, but I will never forget what he looked like. He was a white guy, but his hands and bare feet were black as night, just from being so dirty. He had a long, scraggly brown beard. He looked like he hadn't showered in months, nor had he cared to. He looked at me with the deadest, glassiest eyes you could imagine. They were glazed over and looking at me like he had recognized that something was there, but didn't recognize it to be another human being. He looked like he had been in that stall the entire night doing some sort of drug that I've never even heard of, not even knowing where or who he was.

I have nothing against the homeless. I don't mean the people like me (nothing against them either), but people that are homeless out of need, not choice. In fact, I probably sympathize with them more than most, but the ones that are strung out on drugs scare the shit out of me as I worry that they are so unstable that they could be dangerous. When homeless people talk to themselves, it fucks up my whole day. One time in Santa Monica, a homeless guy looked at me and screamed, "THE BOARD BOARD BOARD, WELL WHO'S THE CHAIRMAN OF THE FUCKING BOARD?!" I was rattled for days on that one, and I definitely didn't know who the chairman of the fucking board was, but I knew that I wanted no part of it. That type of homeless always kind of sticks with me. Alone, in the middle of the night, I got even more shaken up than usual.

I didn't even pee, I just swiftly walked back to my truck, periodically looking over my shoulder to see if he got out of the bathroom and was coming after me. A piece of me wishes I had just knocked so that I didn't have to see this, but the other piece thinks he wouldn't have even responded if I did knock because he was so out of it.

When I got back into the truck, I knew I wasn't going to be able to sleep. My heart was pounding like I had just drank three cold brews after the worst hangover of my life. It was now a matter of just making it to the morning where it would be an acceptable time to be out and about in the daylight and walking around. It wasn't because I was worried he was going to come find me. I was more just shaken by the whole thing and would be thinking about it for hours.

Were this guy and I on the same level now? I was going to the bathroom in the middle of the night, same bathroom as him. I was homeless, same as him. In my mind, this truck thing was just a fun way to get out more and travel and live a simpler life, but in reality, was I just in love with the idea of it? Was what I just saw more like what it was going to be? Were more nights in store of the same and I'd get to be buddies with some of these guys? We would all be hitting the same spots at night in the same way people become regulars at a bar; would I be a regular at a bathroom with the other homeless guys? "Hey Phil," I'd ask another regular, "can I borrow stall six tonight? My go-to is under maintenance." What the fuck was I thinking?

The sad truth was, this was what the normal homelessness looked like. People going to the public bathroom in the middle of the night weren't going to be like me or the guy I had met in the gym parking lot that was living out of his Tundra. Most of the people that were homeless, especially those living in a big city and not in a Bureau of Land Management site or travelling to exotic places, were this type of homeless. According to the National Coalition for the Homeless, a strong ratio of homeless people, 26%, have a drug dependency, and even more have an alcohol dependency. On top of this, about a third of homeless people have a mental illness (Murray, 2018)[9]. So, there are some people dealing with some serious shit out there, much more serious than the anxiety that I face from being lonely or not enjoying my 9-5 as much as I'd like. Reading those stats and seeing it in real life made me feel like such a spoiled brat. A lot of these homeless people were struggling much worse than me and I was worrying that this was the type of life that I wasn't just living, but *choosing*.

It consumed all my thoughts and I started to wonder if all of the naysayers were right. Maybe this was stupid and they all knew the truth and I was just being stubborn and obnoxiously trying to be different. How embarrassing is it going to be when I have to tell all of the people that I told I was doing this, "hey actually, I am not going to live in my truck. I did it for a day and couldn't handle it. It was just a dumb fuckin' idea anyways." I was discouraged and ashamed and I knew everyone was going to ask how the first night went. I could either lie and tell them it went well or tell the truth and say it was one of the longest nights of my life. Seven in the morning came and I was never so happy to get out of bed on a morning that I was as dog shit tired as I was. Night one was in the books.

6

REFUGEE

(0:50)

That morning when I got out of the bed, the first thing I
did was call my brother, Logan. Actually, the first thing I did
was take a piss, at a different public restroom, and then I called
Logan. I told him all about the first night and how I wasn't sure
if this was a complete mistake and that I should just swallow my
pride and give up. He talked me off the ledge and explained to
me that the first night is always tough in a new setting. Logan
had lived in some wild, literally wild, places over the years and
he knew his fair share of tough first nights.

He reminded me of some of his tough firsts and described
how the second was always so much easier. It wasn't because
the second night you've gotten past all of the uneasiness, but it
was because you were so exhausted that you didn't have the
energy to worry. Once I was over the first few nights and my
body just wanted to sleep, it wouldn't matter where I was, or
what would typically keep me up. Eventually, I would get the
sleep simply because my body would find a way. It needed to.

Logan had helped calm me down a lot and gave me some
hope that the whole idea wasn't bad. It was just that change
was typically tough for me. Since I guess you could say that this
was a big goddamn change, maybe I just needed to give myself
a chance to get used to it. I hung around the bay and then
treated myself to the only breakfast I knew during football
season, a burger and beers at Sonny's. It was my Sunday spot,

so if I wanted to get the truck life started on the right foot, on top of trying new things, I had to continue to do the things I already loved doing. The Pats had the 10:00 am game so I got there for kickoff, had a couple of pints, watched them lose to the Panthers, and then went to the beach in hopes of a nap.

I didn't nap, but the beach day was a fine one. It was a beautiful, sunny day in San Diego and I got to swim in the cold Pacific to wake me up, but tire me out all at once. I read a little bit of my book, hung with some friends and got ice cream like we did every Sunday night before getting ready for bed.

When it got late, I asked some of my buddies, "If I can't sleep tonight by around three in the morning, can I come and sleep on your couch? It's just to get me through these first couple of days and since I have work in the morning, I can't go in on two straight nights of no sleep."

The answer I received was a resounding "no" and thank God for it. I'm glad I had pals that weren't going to just let me quit so easily.

"If you're doing this, you're doing this." MC told me, "You're not just going to be half in and half out."

It was the exact response I needed because on night two there wasn't going to be an option to give up just yet. It'd get better; it had to. I moved my truck because I told myself I'd never park in that spot again, and found a different backstreet that was also quiet, but this one had less apartments and more single family residences. This meant that less people would be walking around and less people could possibly see me make the Tacoma Tumble into bed.

I made the climb in and was a little bit smoother with it this time as I had learned from some of my clumsiness from night one. I, again, peered around out the window, moving aside the back curtain, to see if anyone saw my maneuver. Once I realized the coast was clear, I stripped down to the underoos. I tossed and turned for a little bit, mostly stressing about the fact that I wasn't going to sleep, but then the next thing you know, I wake up to the sound of my alarm clock. Logan was right. Between the lack of sleep, IPAs for breakfast, and swimming in the ocean, my body was so beat that I probably could have fallen asleep standing up.

My alarm went off promptly at 05:27, as it would every Monday through Friday while I lived in the truck, and I rolled out. The best part about the early wake up was that almost nobody was up at this hour on the west coast, so nobody was going to see a man wiggling out of his truck shell with bed head. I'd drive to the gym, workout, shower, and be ready to attack the day at work.

The only thing was, I couldn't work out when I got to the gym. Something awful had happened and my mind was elsewhere. This was the morning of the Las Vegas massacre. I got to the 24 Hour fitness and my iPhone popped up with the news alert telling me that over 50 people had been killed and even more had been injured in Las Vegas at a country concert. I immediately texted a friend that I knew was there. She had actually told me she had an extra ticket in the days leading up to the concert and asked if I wanted to go. I told her I couldn't go because I had to move out of my place, and into my truck. She's a wonderful girl, and a very pretty girl that I had a small history with. Under almost any other circumstances, I would have loved to join her, but I had important plans and wanted to start the truck life off on the right foot. As crazy as it may sound, being that I am one of those people that believes everything happens for a reason, moving into the truck could have saved my life. Who knows if I would have been one of the tragic victims had I not been moving and decided to join my friend? I wasn't thinking about that then, though. That thought didn't cross my mind until later in the day. That morning, all of my thoughts were with my friends and the other victims. Fortunately, she was okay. Her friend, however, was in surgery. I had the pleasure of meeting her friend a few times as well. Not that anybody deserves such an awful thing to happen to them, but she seemed like the sweetest girl in the world, so I was devastated to hear that she was one of the gunshot victims.

It was all over the TVs at the gym, the worst massacre in United States history. I was trying to get a light workout in to keep my mind off of it, but I couldn't keep my mind off of the girls and my eyes off of the screen. I tried to get a back workout in, but when that wasn't working and I was just going through the motions, I moved to the treadmill to try to run away from it. The treadmill was just as bad, as it felt like my legs were numb and functioning properly. The workout was useless; I gave up, showered, and headed to work.

Work went by about as slow as it could have. News would trickle in throughout the day from the shooting and a lot of the focus at work was on that. A few coworkers of mine knew people that were at the concert also. It would be a long road, but fortunately, my friend's friend would be okay. Selfishly, I kept imagining if I was there, thankful that I turned down the offer to go, but also feeling guilty. I was wondering, if I had gone, maybe we would have been in a different spot. I knew it obviously wasn't my fault, but that whole butterfly effect thing always freaked me out, so I wondered. On top of all of this running through my head, I was already running on fumes. I had slept okay the previous night, but I was still in sleep debt from the night before. I felt like my eyes were being held open by clothespins, with someone pouring soda in them, and I could have passed out on my keyboard at any moment.

Unfortunately, the victims of the Las Vegas Massacre weren't the only deaths that happened that day. Around lunchtime, Banks sent into our Gin Bandits text group, "RIP Tom Petty." I was hoping that it was one of those fake news things where some asshole spreads around the internet that someone famous died. I don't know what kind of sicko would do it on that day of all days, but unfortunately, it was not a hoax. My second favorite artist, who I was lucky enough to see two weeks before his death, had passed away. I usually don't get emotional over celebrity deaths, but that one, on that day, had me overwhelmed.

By the time work was over, I just wanted to go home, sit on the couch, watch TV and get my mind off of things. One of the most important reasons for moving into the truck was to do less of that, but on a day like today, I thought I needed it. I found, even before I lived in my truck that the best thing to do to get your mind off of things was not the mind-numbing shit, like TV. The stuff that really got you out of your funk was doing the things that were mind-*soothing*. Reading, riding my bike, jumping in the ocean, surfing, or basically anything besides just sitting around feeling sorry for myself, that's what I truly needed to get out of a funk rather than just get through the funk.

I decided to go to the one place always there for me, the beach. I took my orange, flowery Tommy Bahama beach chair, threw my book into one of the zippered pouches, took a water from the cooler in my truck and put it into the pouch in the chair that was supposed to be a cooler, and tossed the straps around my shoulders like a backpack. I had parked by a section of the beach where you take a blacktop path down from the cliff to the sand. It was where the most surfers in my town would go to, so I'd be able to watch them while I read my book. It was also right below the cliff where people did sunset yoga, so sometimes you could look up and see hundreds of people on the cliff Warrior two-ing in a golden glow unison. It was a beautiful and peaceful sight to see. It was certainly a welcoming, calming sight to see that night.

I sat and read until sunset. My heart was still heavy with the events from the day, but I was able to truly clear my head with that magical music of waves on sand and the painting-like colors of the San Diego sunset. It had been a tough day, but I couldn't have imagined a better way to get my mind off of things. I was glad that I didn't spend the night watching SportsCenter at Night (no offense to my man SVP!) for three hours, being in a mental coma every time a commercial came on and I had nothing to drown out my thoughts, and then going to bed to think of all of the awful things that happened in the day. Instead, I was able to appreciate a picturesque sunset, read a healthy chunk of a good book, and watch some fun waves caught by…. well, not me. I know it sounds simple. You don't have to live in your truck to do all of this. I know. It just isn't always as easy to go out and walk the world around you when you have a comfy, cozy cave to go back to.

Night three came and I had found another prime, quiet parking spot to call home for the night. It was a different location than the first couple of nights. I figured it was best to move around and find new streets, never staying on one too often and drawing attention to myself. Night three would be spent up the road from some of my buddies, so I knew the area pretty well, and knew that it was quiet and mostly filled with young adults like myself. I slept pretty decently again. By all accounts, it was getting a little easier each day.

Every night for the rest of that week, I found it easier to make the climb into the truck. I bumped into less things. I banged my head on the roof less. I was finding it easier to fall asleep now that I knew I could do it and people had more to worry about in their lives than whether or not anybody was sleeping in a vehicle outside of their homes.

The gym routine was getting less clunky and taking me less and less time to get ready, get in, and get out. The first couple of days, my backpack was a jumbled mess in the mornings, and it was taking me a while to get ready to workout and then to get ready to shower, and then to get ready for work. By the end of the week, I knew where to keep everything in my backpack for easy access, so that I could get in and out quickly. There was a section of the backpack for clean work clothes, a section for gym shoes (where the dirty clothes would go also after the workout), and a section for my toiletries which were organized in a nice toiletry bag that my sister, Erin, had gotten me for Christmas. I started sleeping in the gym outfit, all clean clothes, that I was going to wear the next day so that I wouldn't have to change twice. When I was little, I used to sleep in my basketball uniform every night before a big game so that I was mentally and physically ready to go the next morning. It felt a little bit like that. My morning routine got more and more dialed and by the end of the week, it felt pretty natural.

The time between the end of the workday and sunset was pretty easy that first week. We hadn't fallen back for daylight savings time yet, so the sun was setting around 18:30 with an afterglow until about 19:00. I usually got home around 17:00, so I had two hours to be outside in the sun. That first week, I either read, rode my bike, or surfed until there was no more light every single day.

Times were a little tougher in the hours between sunset and bed time during that first week. I didn't really know what to do with myself at first. One night, I walked the boardwalk, but the later it got the more the crazies came out. Being alone walking the boardwalk in some of the more dimly lit areas made me a little uneasy, so I didn't really love doing that. Another night, I tried reading on the beach with my book light, but even more of the other type of homeless were out on the beach during those hours. As I'd try to read, I'd hear something behind me, and it would be a homeless person looking for cans and talking to himself, which you know I love. I felt a little vulnerable just being out on the beach without anyone around besides those people. My mind would wander to me getting killed and pushed out to sea never to be found again, so I was a little spooked doing that. I tried going to the gym another night, but I didn't really want to do two-a-days, so my heart wasn't really in the workout. I hadn't really figured out this part of the routine, so I definitely missed the comfort of a couch watching TV during those hours.

That first week, I found that I was just getting into bed early usually around 20:30, with nothing really left to do, or nowhere else to go, I went to where I knew I was safe, or at least as safe as I could be given my circumstances. I was still worrying a lot before bed and keeping myself up for an hour or so, just thinking. Since I was getting up so early and my body was still catching up on sleep, it wasn't too long before I was able to fall asleep and was getting six to eight hours every night. The sleeping was getting easier with each passing night.

I knew that I just had to get through that first work week and then I would get to enjoy the traveling life on the weekend — what I had looked forward to most about truck life. I had to work in Los Angeles on Friday, so I planned on just making a trip of it. I'd leave Thursday night, sleep in Huntington Beach that night, wake up and surf Friday morning, go to L.A. and work until about 14:00, spend the rest of the day in Santa Monica at the beach and then head back to HB for Friday night. I'd wake up Saturday morning and make my way to Venice. Kings of Leon was playing at the Hollywood Bowl, so I'd see them with a friend Saturday night and then make the drive back to San Diego Sunday night. All week, it was something to look forward to. So even at the moments where I had my doubts, and was questioning if I was as crazy as everyone said, I knew that I just had to make it to Thursday night and then the whole week would be worth it. If I wanted to put my tail between my legs and admit defeat after that, at least I got a couple of new cities under my belt out of it.

I didn't know the first thing about Huntington and it'd be the first place that I'd travel to and sleep in that wasn't San Diego. MC lived there before moving to San Diego so I asked him where to sleep.

He replied, in typical ladies' man MC fashion, "A girl I used to bump boots with lived on this quiet street named Jane St. I'd try there." My man was spot on. It was quiet, nobody was stirring around, and it was dark enough so that nobody was going to see me make the climb, but also light enough so that my truck wouldn't get robbed in the middle of the night while I snoozed in the back. By the time I had gotten up there it was already pretty late and I was getting up early, so I just went straight from cab to bed.

I got up early, long before I had to be at the distribution center I was going to for work, and felt that crisp beach air tickling my nose to wake me up to surf. It was small, but clean, fun waves that I rode for a couple hours as the sun came up over the buildings. The rising sun helped to warm the rest of my body up, since my wetsuit was so cold that I was full George Costanza mode downstairs. I still had about another forty five minutes to the DC, so at around 08:00, I got out, rinsed myself off, changed into my warehouse jeans, and hatted up to look just unsloppy enough to pass in a distribution center. To be honest, I probably could have gone even sloppier. As I pulled out of HB, "Backstreets" by Bruce came on my radio and I turned up my Tacoma stereo as loud as it could go, smiling and looking out at the golden road ahead of me, knowing that I was starting to thrive living on the backstreets. It was exactly the type of morning that I had envisioned when I thought about making the move.

After work on Friday, I went to a 24 hour fitness in L.A. and showered to get the warehouse stink off of me. Afterwards, I met up with a friend from high school, Breanna, in Santa Monica. She had lived up there for a year or so, but we didn't see each other as much as I would have liked. She was one of my closest friends from home and only living two hours away, so there wasn't really an excuse as to why I didn't see her more often.

We met up on the beach and spent the day in the sun on beach chairs, catching up. On a normal Friday after work, I would have just gone home sitting in traffic for three hours. Being able to catch up with an old friend instead was icing on the cake to my workday turned surf trip. When the sun set, we walked back to our cars, and mine was closer so we said our goodbyes there. She noticed the shell on the back, but had no idea that this was my new home. I decided not to tell her. She probably wouldn't have understood it, and I wasn't really in the mood to explain it to her for the last half hour that we were together, so we said our fare thee wells and I drove back to Huntington.

I probably could have found somewhere to sleep in Santa Monica or Venice, but since it was my first week and I was a little nervous sleeping places I didn't know, I decided to go back to a place I knew that I could be successful. Huntington was now a safe zone in my mind, so I drove back and slept on a street close to the one I had slept the night before. After another successful night's sleep and another morning surf in Surf City, U.S.A., I rinsed myself off, hopped into my truck and made the drive back up to Venice.

I had never been to Venice, so I was excited to see it. Specifically I was excited to see Hank Moody's house. I had the pleasure of meeting the real life Hank, David Duchovny, earlier in the year. I saw him in New York City, where Hank's character was the most in his element. I was 99.9% sure it was him, but it wasn't until he finally passed me that I called out in the most timid voice, "D-david Duchovny…" and he turned and gave me a wave to acknowledge that it was him. It was at this point that I couldn't contain myself any longer, and shouted out, "OH MY GOD PLEASE!!" and ran him down like the fanboy I was and got a picture with him. It was one of the best moments of 2017. So, yeah, I was excited to see Venice.

Another one of my friends lived there, so I was visiting her and was going to stay at her place on Saturday night. She was working in the morning, so I was able to explore the whole morning by myself and see all of the things that she was probably sick of showing friends that were visiting. There is nothing worse than having to drag your friend around to all of the touristy shit in their town that they have seen a thousand times. I walked the canals that Hank and Becca used to walk in *Californication*, and went to the house that his character lived in. I walked the boardwalk and took in the Venice vibe.

When my friend got off around lunch time, we went out to lunch and then hit the beach for a few hours. After the beach, we went back to her place and showered and got ready for the show. We headed into West Hollywood, or We-Ho as the kids say, and went to a trendy rooftop bar. "I feel so L.A." I told her, much to her annoyance. Afterwards, we went to see one of my three favorite living bands, Kings. They put on one of the best sets that I could have imagined with all of my favorites, excluding "Pickup Truck," and the Hollywood Bowl was a sick venue. There is nothing like watching one of your favorite bands with the sunset coming down behind the mountains as they tower over the stage in the background.

A surf trip in Huntington at a new break, catching up with old friends, trendy new bars in new cities, and seeing one of my favorite bands put on a killer show made for an A+ first weekend in Taco. The fact that I was getting all of the gas that it took me to drive up to L.A. paid for by my company anyways, plus the fact that I slept in my truck two nights and at a friend's place the third night made the A+ weekend an A++, since it was basically a free trip. This whole truck thing could be even easier than I thought.

7

BLUE SKY

(0:35)

Joshua Tree was one of the top places in California that I wanted to go. I'd been living in San Diego for two years and just a couple of hours away, but I hadn't made it yet. There and Vegas were the two places that my friends and I would always say we were going to go to, but then we could never find a weekend that worked for everyone. The idea always eventually fizzled out. So now that I was living in my truck and could travel any weekend I wanted, I was going to go.

If nobody else wanted to join, I would go alone, and I told my friends as much. To my surprise, one by one they decided they wanted to come. MC was in first, so I thought we were going to have ourselves a little bromance in the desert. I was delighted to hear there would be no *Brokeback Mountain* whisperings behind mine and MC's backs — not that there's anything wrong with that — when our other friend, Dave, told me that he was in too. Once Dave was in, he invited another one of his buddies, Mikey. One of my closest friends and former roomates, Ryan was the last of the boys to join the squad, so now we had a full group of five fellas heading into the desert.

I had told Soph about the trip and she was in, but then, in typical Soph fashion, she had to bail because she was going to have to work on Saturday. Soph was the girl I had gone to see Kings of Leon with in Venice, and by all accounts, one of the most captivating people I have ever had the pleasure of meeting. A few of my friends had met her at a music festival and said that she was the "biggest homie of a girl" that they knew. I didn't buy into the hype until I met her, but when I did, I was the conductor of the hype train. She fit the bill. She lived up to it all and more. We connected instantly and became the type of friends that felt like they'd known each other for twenty years, when in reality we'd only known each other for a month.

Going to a place like Joshua Tree, you wouldn't want to bring a girl that was going to complain the whole time about how hot it was, or how far she had to hike. You wanted to bring a gamer, and Soph was just that. She was down to earth in a way that was refreshingly authentic. So, she was the only girl that I had asked. With all of the things I love about her, she can be a bit of a flake, so when she said that she was coming, I half expected another text explaining to me why she actually couldn't come. That is unfortuately exactly what happened. When I got that text saying she couldn't make it, I wasn't surprised or totally upset because I still had more than the party of one, me, to head to Joshua Tree with and I would have been happy even if it was just me.

What I did not expect was the un-flake. I got another text from her on Thursday night saying, "Wanna hear something tight, not working this weekend. Jean and I wanna hike, maybe we crash?" Talk about a turn of events. I went from going solo, to going with a couple guy friends, to going with a squad of dudes, to going with a squad of dudes plus two beautiful ladies. I should just say I'm going on trips alone more often, in hopes that other people will join.

Friday night, we hit Ralph's, the grocery store, and did the classic, "buy a shit ton of food, but buy no food" move. We got some sandwich stuff, some s'more stuff, and the beef jerky/nuts type of snacks that you need for hiking. We bought some water, but Ryan and I knew we would need more than what we got. We both drank a shit ton of it and the amount we were getting wouldn't be enough for a normal day, let alone a day of hiking in the sun. We grabbed some firewood too and were for the most part ready to go. We packed all the stuff into the fridge at MC and Dave's house and put my cooler out to be loaded in the morning.

I went to sleep that Friday night jacked up for the weekend, with no stress about my truck life. It had gotten me to take this trip and I was about to have a sweet time with a phenomenal crew. I parked outside of the boys' house and slipped into bed pretty early. I was packed for the trip, as I was packed for every day of my life, with everything beneath my bed. I had the cooler inside ready to be packed up, the popup tent from my storage container in Dave's truck bed, and my beach chair, which would become my campfire chair, in its usual spot in the cab of the truck.

When I woke up, I immediately had those pre-trip jitters where you wake up and don't hit snooze once, don't lay around at all, just get up and get ready to tackle the trip; the kind of jitters you get the first day of camp in the summer growing up or the morning of a big tailgate in college. It's the type of jitters you wish you could have every single morning when you wake up. But at the same time, the fact that those instances are so rare make them that much better when they do happen. It was around 04:00 so I didn't have to worry about anyone seeing me make the hop out of the bed, so I wiggled out and started packing the food into the cooler.

We were whispering in the house to not wake up the other roommates, but the type of loud whisper that you do when you're fired up about something and can't be expected to keep it at a reasonable volume.

Once everything was in the trucks, we headed out of San Diego around 04:30, still before the sun was up. We wanted to make sure that we got there as early as possible because the campsite we were going to was first come, first serve. Envisioning us getting there and not having a campsite, my stress levels were through the roof. It was one thing if I would have gotten there alone and there weren't any campsites. I could just spend all day hiking in Joshua Tree, with the truck in a lot in the park, and then at the end of the day head to a place right outside of the park and let the Tahoma reside there for the night. For me, it would be not too much different than my normal life. But with all eight of the other people coming, if we didn't get a campsite, we were so screwed. We'd have to turn around, having wasted a Saturday morning, or pray that a campground outside of the park had vacancy. Even so, that wouldn't be the same and it would be a total bitch getting everyone in and out and ready at the same time, especially with the lack of cell service we were going to have.

I had to stay positive though and not think like that. MC was in my truck and Dave and Ryan drove in Dave's truck with Mikey's Jeep behind him. Mikey was going to a Dodger's game the next day and since Soph and Jean were driving from LA, we would need two campsites with three cars anyway, so a fourth car didn't hurt. MC and I had Seger, Springsteen, Joel, and other old favorites geared up to play the whole way, so vibes were high. I'll never forget the sun coming up over the mountains that morning with "Roll Me Away" practically blowing out my speakers at full blast with the windows down and fat smiles stretched across both of our faces. We thought that we were in for a hell of a weekend.

That is, until we actually got to the park. We pulled up to the south entrance, courtesy of my printed maps from Google Maps, around 07:45 - 08:00. We pulled into the little visitor entrance building and asked the woman, "Hey are there any campsites still available?" Hoping she'd say, "Yeah! There's a fuck ton, just come on in and park where ever!"

Instead she replied, "Oh. Today? I don't think so today. It's Saturday. Most of the spots are taken Friday night for the weekend and the park was completely full last night. You can go in and try, but I'm not sure you'll find anything"

This was my biggest fear of the trip. All of these people were going to drive all this way, pack their shit up for the day, look forward to a sweet time in the desert. What they were going to get instead was a big let down, courtesy of PFG and a three hour drive back.

For the next hour we went in and out of Joshua Tree looking for our friends and trying to call them. Vibes were low and MC and I were starting to lose hope. We were driving through this amazing area with enormous boulders and tree species I had never seen before, but we couldn't even appreciate it because we were so blown that we had driven all this way to have to turn back around. We pulled up to Jumbo Rocks campground and sure enough who do we see? My man Ryan walking up the road. They had found a campsite! No, they had found two! I had never been so happy that, although I was a slow driver, my friends were not.

All of my worries dissipated and now I could finally enjoy these vast desert views. We had one campsite up the road from the one that all of my friends were setting up at. That one didn't have any cars there at the moment, just a lone tent protecting our land from any other potential campers looking for a spot. I pulled up my truck and parked it right in front of the site marker and we had officially staked our claim to two excellent campsites. Things were looking up.

I walked down the road and passed a few other campers, gave my hellos. I noticed a black thing in the middle of one of the paths so I walked over to it to see what it was. There were trees and rocks all around, but we weren't out in the middle of the wilderness; this was a path I imagined was beaten daily from campers going from camp to camp or camp to trail. When I got over there, I wasn't expecting anything like what I saw. It was a fat, hairy tarantula. I'm kind of standing there looking at it watching it walk along and thinking to myself, "Is this just normal? How come nobody else is over here looking at this? Why aren't people freaking out like they do when they see a harmless Daddy Longlegs?" I was blown away because this was something I thought I'd only see in the movies or in a pet store, but no, this thing was just cruising around looking for his buddies or some grub probably. It was some Nat-geo shit in real life and the trip continued to get better.

Everyone was setting up camp and mine, as always, was immediately ready to go. It wasn't camp though since my home had just been relocated. I decided I'd try to get comms up and call the Soph to see if she was close. We had no way of telling them where we were, and we were in the middle of the desert, so I was a little worried she wasn't going to find us. She knew what kinds of cars we had and which campground we were at, but I wanted to make sure that she was able to get to us. There is absolutely nothing worse than when you are lost and trying to call the person you are trying to get to and they aren't picking up.

I climbed the tallest boulder I could find and sure enough had the smallest of bars on my phone. I sent a text, but it wasn't going through. I tried the holding the phone to the chin trick, the "hold the extra two feet above your head because that will definitely work" trick, but all to no avail. I felt like that traitor piece of garbage from the Sprint commercials that used to say for Verizon, "Can you hear me now?" At this point, the girls would either find us or hopefully find another spot and camp separately from our group. The fellas were all done setting up camp, so we put some sandos down our gullets, got our packs together and got ready for a hike.

I had never gone on a hike that wasn't on or near a trail. I love going off the beaten path on a hike, but there's always a path to come back to should I want to use it. Here, that was not the case. There were hiking paths that you could walk to and see the touristy stuff that it's known for, but we didn't want that. We decided, let's just walk west. So that's what we did.

We walked for miles just climbing peaks of boulders and then going down valleys to go back up another peak of boulders. We got so far that we could no longer see camp. We knew that if we wanted to go back, all we had to do was walk east and we'd eventually be able to find a landmark or something to get us back to the site, but there was definitely a little worry that we'd get lost in the middle of the desert. Apparently, it happens more often than you think.

It was my favorite hike I had ever been a part of, just guys being dudes. We were climbing rocks that we had no business climbing, treating the earth like it was our jungle gym. The fellas were pushing each other to do some sketchy climbs that we probably lacked the experience for, grabbing a hold of rocks and pulling ourselves up while acting like we knew what we were doing. It was a blast though, and got all of our adrenaline pumping. You'd get to one of the peaks and look out and just see desert, no buildings, no people, no airplanes or roads - just the great outdoors and it was beautiful in a different type of beautiful that I had never experienced. There was no blue water in the distance or a city skyline to look out to. Joshua Tree was just rocks and literal Joshua Trees with a goldish-brown glow all over from the sun beating down on them all day.

One of the first peaks we got to, we saw a coyote running towards something across the valley below, thankfully not in our direction. It was some more Nat Geo shit in real life and we were all pretty blown away by it. He was running pretty swiftly with a determined stride as if he was going to find his dinner, or maybe going to find a mate, but whichever it was, we were happy to be watching from above. We waited a few minutes up there for him to get a little further away.

The end goal was always to get to the top of this rock formation that we could see from early on in the hike because it was the tallest one on the horizon. Finally we had gotten to the base of it and it was a lot more vertical than we had anticipated. We would have to do some real climbing to get to the top, but we were cruising, with so much testosterone floating in the air, you could practically smell the pheromones. On a normal day, we may have pussied out and said let's try to find another peak, but we felt invincible on this day, so we went for it.

We had to contort our bodies in ways that we weren't used to and grab onto slabs of rock that would make our forearms burn from squeezing so hard with just our fingertips. I may be exaggerating a little, because we weren't going full on *Meru*. For inexperienced climbers, though, this was definitely pushing the limits just enough where it was still safe, but could have turned for the worse if we were careless.

We finally got to the top of the plateau and the 360 degree view around Joshua Tree was spectacular. It felt like we were the kings of the world, or at the very least kings of Joshua Tree because this had to be the highest point. Chests pounding, breath heavy, and hands scraped up and trembling a little from the force we had to use to grab the rocks, we stood up there sucking in the cleanest air. There was nothing but the great outdoors and the fellas.

I looked out and thought to myself that this was the quietest I had ever heard nature in my life. I had been in quieter rooms, maybe during the SAT in high school, but never had I heard so much sublime silence with the sun on my face. There were no horns honking, no music blaring, and no basic bitches/Chad and Brads screaming about how perfect the views were or how gram-worthy of a picture they had just taken like you could almost guarantee you'd get with such a breathtaking view. There weren't even any rivers flowing or birds chirping; it was completely silent. As I'm thinking this, MC is saying something to the other fellas that I had tuned out because I was so blown away by this noiseless tranquility.

MC was standing to my left, so without saying a word to break the silence, I tapped his right hip with my left hand and pointed to my ear to tell him to listen for a second. He does it and once he gets the same feeling that I got, he taps the rest of the boys and tells them the same thing saying, "yo, shh for a second. Listen." We stood there for about thirty seconds all listening to the silence, amazed that we could hear this anywhere, let alone here. Each of us were looking out into the horizon, breathing calmly, smiling the type of smile you get when all of your worries seem so far away and all that matters is the present. Our present at that time could not have been more ideal. It was so much cooler and less corny than it sounds, but by the time it was over MC finally breaks the silence with a, "Damn. That was sick!" It was, it was one of the most surreal moments of my life.

Hungry for some more sandos, and running low on water, we decided to head back east. We got back to camp and there was another car parked at our site. Who the hell is parking in our campsite? It wasn't Soph's red Jeep Wrangler, so I was a little perturbed as to who would be trying to bunk up with us. Spots were running low, so if someone seemed like they weren't going to kill us in our sleep and just needed a place to set up shop for the night, I'm sure we'd be fine with it. I didn't see anyone around though, so I was curious.

For the next couple hours we sat around the picnic table, swapping stories, making sloppy sandwiches, playing some can-jam, and reminiscing on the best hike of our lives. The best part was that nobody was on their phones. Why would you be unless you were addicted to Doodle Jump or something? There was no service, so no need to be on your phone. Everyone was able to just stay in the moment and enjoy the company and the scenery.

After a few hours, from the east, opposite of where we had hiked, we see a few hikers walking towards us. This must have been the people with the car. Sure enough, it was Soph, Jean, and Jean's weekend date, Bobby. It was Jean's car. Stupid, PFG! Here I was still worrying that they just hadn't found us and turned back and at the same time worrying about a random car that was at our campsite. Couldn't put that one together, huh, Watson?

We chilled for a few more hours at the campsite and when the sun was starting to go down, we packed a few Pacifico cans into our backpacks and went to one of the closer peaks than where we had gone before. San Diego gets golden hour, but this was a golden hour like I hadn't seen. With the brown of the rocks, getting hit by the bright yet fading sun reflecting into the air, it felt like we were living in a movie shot in sepia tone. Cold Pacificos, hot rocks to sit on, a cool breeze coming in to counter the sizzling sun, vibes couldn't be higher. We took some pictures, like the type of people I had complained about a few paragraphs ago, but we had to right? The smiles in those pictures were so genuine. In fact, a smile couldn't leave my face that night.

We got back to camp and built a fire - teepee not log cabin, obviously. The last of the food was s'mores stuff and some weiners to roast over the fire; it sounded like a perfect dinner to me. We sat around the flames for a few hours drinking a few more Pacificos and getting to that perfect buzz since nobody was out there looking to get white girl wasted.

We played a drinking game passing around the whiskey, called, "you're a bitch if you haven't…" which is basically the reverse of never have I ever. It ended with MC telling us you're a bitch if you haven't pooped your pants and then going on to tell us the story of him soiling himself during soccer practice as a little kid and his buddy's dad making him sit in the bed of the truck on the carpool home. I was thinking thank god that no poopy-pants ever sat in my truck bed, which now doubled as my home...

It was a long day that started at 04:00 of driving, hiking, and having the sun beat down on us, so after a while around the fire, we called it a night pretty early. The goal was to get up early to watch the sunrise, so going to bed early was probably the right idea.

Soph, Jean, Bobby, and I started to walk back to the other campsite up the road. I had assumed that those three would sleep in the three person tent that they had brought and I would sleep at home. As we're walking up to the campsite, Jean and Bobby trailed back to walk just the two of them and Soph walked up closer to me and said, "Hey is anyone else sleeping in your truck with you?"

I wanted to look around and say, "Soph, who the hell else would be sleeping in my truck with me tonight? Believe it or not, Joshua Tree Tinder isn't exactly popping off and none of the fellas would want to, nor would fit, in the truck with me." I laughed and told her that no, nobody else was and she asked if she could. Of course, she could.

She was the perfect first girl to sleep in the truck with me for a few reasons. Soph was the first girl that I told I was living in my truck. When I went up to Venice the weekend before, we had met up and I nervously told her. We knew each other a little, but not well enough where I could tell her this and expect her to know me well enough not to think that I was a bum or a serial killer just living in my truck, creeping around town. I told her in an awkward, embarrassed, rationalizing way. Even though I wasn't embarrassed about it and had explained it to my guy friends before, it felt hard telling a girl I had a slight crush on, not knowing what to expect her reaction would be.

When I initially told her, she responded, "oh that's cool." I didn't know if she actually thought it was cool or if she was just being polite, so I kept over explaining trying to tell her all of the reasons I was doing it, all I wanted to get out of it, all I wanted to see and that I knew it was crazy. She stopped me. She said something that I'll never forget because from then on, I didn't feel like I had to justify it to anyone. The people that I wanted to understand most, the people that I connected with instantly, the people that were the best type of people in my life, they understood. She said, "you don't have to justify it to me. I actually think it's really cool. If you were living in the middle of nowhere doing it, that'd be one thing. But you like to surf and live in a hip beach town and just want to be outside, I think that's awesome." That was one of the biggest weights off of my shoulders, and it meant more than she could ever know.

She was also perfect for the truck bed because she was five feet tall. Actually, she was four feet eleven and three quarters. You'd never know because she had a confidence and swagger like she was a six foot badass. I only know her height because one time I asked her, just curious, how tall she was and she adorably said, "Five foot... well actually four-eleven and three quarters, but I like to round up." The truck bed was only five feet long, so she wouldn't even have to sleep diagonally like I did every night.

I had showed her the truck in Venice, and again when she first got there because Jean was curious and they both thought it was really cool, or at least that's what they said. They were particularly impressed with the shelves I had built, which I was impressed with myself on, and liked my "decorations" (aka the tapestry that served as my blinds). Since she had already seen it, I knew that she knew what she was getting herself into and was willingly ready to crawl up in to that small space and get more cozy with PFG than anyone would probably want to be. So, I popped the shell open and helped her in first, being careful to make sure that she didn't bang her head on the roof as I so often did in the early days. Then, I hopped in myself.

It took some getting used to with two people in there and we had to kind of wiggled around to finally find a position where we were both comfortable. It reminded me a bit of freshman year of college, when you would try to sleep with a girl in your little twin bed, trying not to wake up your roommate. I bumped into the tapestry at one point, knocking part of it down and having it fall on us, so I had to quickly fix it before we both felt even more claustrophobic than she probably felt already. Then, we ruined the whole comfortable position because we turned and faced each other to have a bedside chat before we went to sleep.

I started joking with her about the last time she was in San Diego, wasted, and made a pass at me. She was visiting MC at the time and was probably going to sleep in his bed, not to mention she was tossed, so I didn't make a move back that night. I was beginning to explain to her the conversation we drunkenly had that night. She stops me, "Please stop, I hate being told what I said when I was drunk," a sentiment I couldn't agree more strongly with. "What... did I tell you how I had a big crush on you?"

That was basically exactly what she had told me that night in San Diego, but I tried to ease her post-drunk anxiety by telling her, "No, it wasn't bad at all, it was nothing." It was nice to hear her say it soberly though. We had a few Pacificos, but we were by no means on the level we were that night, so this seemed like confirmation that there was a little spark there.

The truck was as dark as a basement at midnight on that night. It was always pretty dark, but in the middle of nature, with no street lights to illuminate the truck through the tapestry, it was even darker than usual. Only the light from the moon and stars was barely shining through. She was talking about something else and I said, "where's your face? Keep talking..." and she kept talking and when I finally found what I believed to be her face, I pulled her in and kissed her.

"That was a smooth move," she said with her big beautiful smile that I couldn't see, but could hear. Little did she know, I thought it was the least smooth move ever, I was literally just trying to find her face. There wasn't a ton of room to operate in there, so I did the best that I could with my movements and we kept fooling around for a little bit, but it wasn't long before we were trying to get comfortable again and I was big spoon.

In the middle of the night, I woke up and could tell something was off. "Are you okay?" I asked.

"Yeah, are you hot?" she replied. She was cute about it and didn't want to directly tell me that she was burning up and probably freaking out in this little space. I couldn't have been less hot. In fact, I was a little cold. I was in one layer, and she was bundled up in every one of the layers she had brought and laying under the blanket.

I felt so bad that she was probably so uncomfortable and may not have told me if I never asked. I told her that it did get hot in there sometimes, but since we were camping it wouldn't matter if we slept with the hatch open. It would basically be the same as sleeping in a tent, and it's not like anybody would bother us out here. I kicked it open.

I was freezing that night. With my one layer on, I big spooned the Soph so hard to try to stay warm. She asked me in the morning if I was cold and I told her I was. She told me she could definitely tell. I guess the big spoon death grip didn't go unnoticed, but we laughed it off. I explained to her that I was wearing about half the clothes she was and she said that, when the hatch was open, she was a perfect temperature. We were a little misaligned on the timing of our comfortability, but it was still a delightful night of sleep with the lights from the stars, the cool breeze and the warm, snuggled up Soph.

We got up at around 05:30 to give us some time to watch the sunset. We hit the campground bathroom, which smelled like absolute buttcheeks, and then met up with Jean and Bobby. We walked over to a nice little valley where the sun would rise over some rocks in front of us. Soph and Jean wrapped up in blankets and sweatshirts and we sat there watching the red sun come over the horizon. It was still a little cold, but getting warmer by the minute.

It was one of the most serene mornings that I could remember. I'd just had one of the best twenty four hours of my life with my boys and some incredible girls. It wasn't everyday that I woke up next to a gorgeous girl, let alone a girl that I was stoked to be waking up next to and thrilled to talk to in the morning. This was a girl that had everything I wanted and she wanted to sleep with me for everything that I was. She was willing to sleep in my little five by four box and tough out the heat and the cold. I didn't have to be the second best version of anyone else when I was with the Soph, like I felt I had to be with other girls in my past. I just had to be the best version of myself, and it made my mindset over the truck life and just women in general feel more at peace. Not every girl was going to understand me or my lifestyle, and that's fine because you never know. The type of girls that you want to understand you the most, they will.

If you're thinking that this story is going to end with the Soph and I getting married and living in the back of the Tacoma happily ever after, I'll end your notion right here. She ended up getting back together with her off again and on again boyfriend, who will now probably be on again forever. I mean it when I say this, the guy is as good of a guy that you could ask for to date your friend. I would never ever say something like that about a past crush's new guy if it weren't wholeheartedly true, but he is a complete stud and I'm proud to call him my friend, not just my friend's boyfriend. He probably knows she's kissed a couple of us at one time or another, but he is still so genuine to us and knows it didn't mean anything.

It wasn't the fact that it was her that slept with me, it was the idea of her. The idea of a girl like that wanting to sleep with me even with my current lifestyle. We're still close friends and that's now all that I look at her as, but that one night she wasn't a friend, she wasn't a crush, she was a hope for the woman I'd eventually find. I still had it in me to connect with a girl like that, truly beautiful inside and out. I just hadn't found my right one, but now I believed I could... and I would.

8

SIMPLE MAN

(2:32)

Ten hours, Taco, me, and the open road. That was what I had in front of me that Wednesday before Thanksgiving. I had been looking forward to the trip for weeks. My first big haul with the home on wheels was bound for Lake Tahoe to snowboard for two days and then to Santa Barbara to surf about halfway to home before driving back to San Diego.

I packed up the cab of my truck to about as filled as she could get. I had my surfboard and snowboard going across the passenger seat to the seat behind the driver seat and my cooler packed up with some sandwich fixins behind the passenger seat. On the passenger seat floor was some of my snowboarding clothes that I would need in a plastic tub so that I could put them in there at the end of the day without soaking up, and stinking up, my whole truck. The thing would have smelled like a high school locker room after a couple days if not for that tub. You know that awful smell of wet plus sweat plus snow plus dirt plus nut sack that you get when you walk into a men's locker room? That was what I wanted to avoid. To be honest it still stunk, but at least it was somewhat contained.

This was going to be my first Thanksgiving away from my family and I knew I had to do it big if I didn't want to be homesick. I wanted to go home, see my best friends, relax with the family, and of course get the post Thanksgiving sandwich. My pop made the best one, the kind where you just mash all the leftovers together and then slap it between two slices of sourdough. It sounds easy, but my father made it into an art. I promise it was the best. I was sad I was missing all of that, but I would be going home for a couple of weeks at Christmas and I figured this was a perfect opportunity to drive up the west coast to northern parts of California that I'd never seen but always wanted to.

It helped that I bought an Epic Pass that year to get unlimited snowboarding at some of the major ski resorts in the US for one flat rate. It pushed me to go as often as I could and since the season was just starting, what better way to start it off than a road trip up to beautiful Lake Tahoe? I had to get a jump on the long drive out of work early. Otherwise, I'd have to stop somewhere half way and crash and then drive the rest in the morning. Being a stubborn, never ask for directions, piss your pants before stopping any more than you need to for pee breaks kind of man, I had no desire to stop along the way. I was going to make it all the way to Tahoe that night.

I got out of work that day and sprinted to my truck without looking back, just like back in my Hooters days, and got ready for the haul. I left around 14:30, so 00:30 was the goal and with a little gas station coffee (sneaky dank!) I knew that I could make that. I had a top notch road trip playlist ready to roar through the sound system and a few podcasts on tap, so I really wasn't dreading the drive at all.

Thing is, I almost like driving alone on long car rides more than I like driving with other people, depending on the people. Sometimes you'll be driving with a group and all they keep talking about is "When are we gonna get there?"; "How much longer?"; "This car stinks like shit"; "I'm hot"; and "I'm cooold." When everyone else starts bitching about it, you even start to kind of get this sense of, "yeah, you know what? This car does fucking stink like shit! I am sweating up a storm back here, too!" and "I just want to be there." Then, everyone is in a horrendous mood. When you're alone, you've got your own thoughts, which I'd grown to be a little more at peace with, your own tunes, and you can appreciate the scenery all around you. I looked at it like, if I was flying home right now, it would probably stink even worse, I'd probably be more uncomfortable and everyone else on the plane would be complaining, or complaneing as I like to say. With all that going on around me, I too would probably be a curmudgeon.

So I pressed play and let it shuffle. "Born to Run" starts me off. What more could you ask for out of the start to the road trip? Followed up by some Petty, Zeppelin, Stones, Jimmy Buffet, Clapton, Bob Seger, Kings of Leon, and Van Morrison. I was groovin'. I made a few phone calls to talk to old friends and the next thing you know, four hours had already gone by. There are few things more sensational than that sense of adventure when you are starting a trip. Whether you're in a car driving out of town with buddies or looking out the plane window as it's taking off, visualizing what kind of new stories you're going to come back with, you are always going to have those pre trip jitters. That feeling always gives me the chills and I had it just about the whole first four hours.

After my excitement started to wear off, I needed something to keep me going and awake at the wheel, so I made the switch to podcasts. A buddy of mine had recommended The Joe Rogan Experience, and a few that I listened to were just okay. I felt like sometimes he could be a little too much for me, but I had just finished *The Perfect Storm* by Sebastian Junger and saw that he was on the podcast, so I gave JRE another shot. Junger also directed *Restrepo* and wrote the book *Tribe*, so he had a wealth of knowledge on the topics of survival and group mentality.

His podcast episode on JRE was all about the tribe mentality. It was about surviving and how people yearn to be a part of a group. Going back to our primal days, that sense of being a part of a group made people feel safe and accepted, which were the top priorities in a much more dangerous world than the world we live in today. People found happiness being a part of a group because their most important task was surviving and the group was successful in that together. He had one bit that stuck with me that day and still does to this day. He said:

> The problem with affluent modern society is it takes away all of the tasks of survival ... No one in this room (I don't think) is having to figure out every morning how to literally physically survive ... The downside is you don't get the sense of mastery over your circumstances ... You don't feel like you are earning your own survival in the world. You feel like it's being handed to you ... That kind of life is correlated with depression ... The suicide rate is rising fastest among middle aged white men, who if you listen to some people, are apparently, arguably the demographic that are most privileged in this society (Rogan & Junger, 2017).[9]

That was me. I come from an affluent neighborhood, I had a good job, I had an unbelievable, loving family and a strong support network of friends. I knew, fully, that I was truly blessed and millions, probably even billions of people in this world would give anything to trade positions with me, but over the years I had still battled extended bouts of depression. I longed for that sense of purpose, the feeling that I was doing something that mattered, the ability to live my life to the fullest. When I couldn't get that sense of purpose and I felt lonely, I'd get depressed and the more I just sat around and sulked, the more time I had to think about my loneliness and my lack of purpose.

Living in the truck gave me that sense of survival and brought me back to that primal state of just longing to make it to the next day. I fully understand that what I was going through by choosing to live in my truck was completely different than the things that people did in tribes and what the people in *Restrepo* had to struggle through. It was a similar feeling, just on a much, *much* smaller scale. Every night finding a safe place to sleep and finding ways to fill my day doing things that I liked made me feel like I was injected with purpose. Instead of being all mopey, sitting in the house watching TV, thinking about what can I do to be more successful in life or how can I get richer, I was worried about which backstreet I was parking on that night. Was it safe and away from the bars, so that no drunk driver would hit me? Was it quiet enough so that I could easily fall asleep? My worries became much simpler, as did my life. I wasn't strapped for cash or running from enemies, but I was still seeking safe shelter and looking for ways to step outside of my comfort zone to find things that I enjoyed, which in a way was a pursuit of survival. Every morning I would wake up having a feeling of guilty pleasure that this thing I was doing made it through another night. It was like I was cheating on the test, but was not getting caught and I kept on getting by. The more I got used to living in the truck, the more I enjoyed doing it, because I was mastering it. I was finding the best place to sleep at night, I was finding my favorite restaurants by exploring places that I wouldn't have splurged on before. I got to know this town like I wouldn't have otherwise and even though I was homeless, I felt more at home than ever before. Sure enough, like Junger said I would be, I was truly happier.

It was just like living at the beach during those summers in college. Again, I was not running from the enemies... except for the guy who used to date that dream girl from the summer of 2013. He was 6'5 and scary, and I would have to avoid him like the plague whenever we were at the same party, but he was not like an enemy that Junger was talking about. I was not going to literally starve, and I had a roof over my head. So, I was surviving just fine. But living like that beach bum was in its own way a sense of surviving, and it was also one of the happiest times of my life. The beers always tasted colder when I knew I had earned them by saving my money eating those cheap meals. Now, in the truck, the bed always felt more comfortable knowing that I had built it and had found my own way of living in it.

Next thing you know, I was driving through one of my favorite places, Mt. Whitney, the highest mountain in the contiguous United States. The previous year I had climbed it with a few buddies. Ordinarily, I don't think it's a crazy tough hike, but when we had gone there was snow everywhere, so the chute was covered in ice. We had to climb it with crampons, which was a big deal for an inexperienced hiker like myself. It was one of the most rewarding experiences of my life getting to the top.

I won't lie to you: I literally shit my pants when I got up there because I was so dehydrated and had eaten only eaten beef jerky and Clif Bars all day. As embarrassing as it is to say, the accident also gives me a strange sense of pride. I can say with full certainty, nobody in the history of time has taken a poo as high up as I had in the contiguous United States. I had to take my underoos off and put them in my poop bag and climb down comando, but at least I have a place in the history books.

Anyways, driving through there was special because it brought me back to those cherished memories. It also brought me back to Junger's idea of being a part of a group. That whole hike up, we all had some very low and shitty points, pun intended, but pulling each other along and encouraging one another to get to the summit was the type of camaraderie that I loved. It's the same type of camaraderie that Junger talked about in the podcast, that people naturally craved. I was spending a lot of time alone living in the truck, but at the same time I had my own little communities. I went to the gym everyday, so the other regulars knew me and would bullshit with me in the morning, which was always a nicer start to the day than a lonely commute to a job I didn't love. I was going to yoga and meeting nice people that were always so friendly and had a big sense of community there. I was seeing some of the same people in the water surfing and starting to get recognized as a guy that could hang and who people could catch waves with rather than the kook that was going to cut you off and take your head off with his wavestorm (yes, that kook was 100% me 2 years before). Taco life was both giving me more peace with being alone and giving me this sense of being part of groups, so I'd say so far it was a success.

Around 23:00, I was starting to get a little sleepy, and it was too late to get another cup of joe unless I want to be up until 03:00. I don't drink a lot of coffee, so when I do, I feel like Bradley Cooper from *Limitless*, which is awesome, but when I'm trying to fall asleep, I'm more like *Rain Man* trying to solve math problems in my head and I cannot get a wink. I thought about pulling over, but I also just wanted to get there. Blaring tunes and sticking head out the window to blast my eyes with wind whenever I got tired was my decision.

I make it to Tahoe right around 00:30, just like I had planned and had to pee like a racehorse. I went into the casino, take a tinkle, and put a tenner on black. What was I supposed to do, not bet? I won and the weekend was off to a killer start. Now came the question of where the hell was I going to sleep? This was one of the first times I was really out of town and out of my element, so I wasn't too sure on the answer to that question. The move, I had read online, was to park in one of the parking lots of the casinos. They'd think you're just a degenerate gambler there from midnight to 08:30 blowing your big money away on the slots and your little money, singles, away on the local ladies of the night at one of the various strip clubs. Who am I to judge? All of that was completely legal in Nevada, but sleeping in your car was not, so maybe I was the degenerate. The forums all said park towards the back and nobody will bother you, so that was what I did. I brushed my teeth and took out my contacts in one parking spot inside the massive parking garage and then moved to my campsite, the back of the casino parking lot.

I hopped out of the cab of the truck, peeped around to see if any of the casino security was lurking around, and then hopped on into bed. I got my seven and a half hours of sound sleep and sure enough I wake up the next morning with no tow, no ticket, just a tall mountain and a lake as blue as Mallorca waters staring me in the face. It was time to "send it" as the kids are saying these days.

The first lift opened at 09:00, so I woke up with thirty to spare. I head into the kitchen, my cooler in the cab of my truck, and make myself lunch. On the menu for that day was a PB&J, turkey sando, and some trail mix. Meanwhile, I ate my breakfast, a protein bar and guzzled down some water from the big jug in my cooler, with drops splashing all down my beard.

Changing into snowboard clothes is never fun. You always get hot and claustrophobic and frustrated that your goddamn zipper gets stuck, so changing in the truck was going to be even more hell. I slipped on my long johns banging into every corner of my truck and decided, I'd had enough. I was going to change outside, in the open. It wasn't that cold, so once I had some pants on it really didn't matter that I changed everything else outside in front of everyone. Did I get some funny looks? Sure, but for the most part everyone got the struggle of putting on snow clothes, so I got a lot more nods of saying, without saying anything, "hey man, I get it. Good luck."

After I got all changed in the parking lot, looking as homeless as I was, I tightened up my boots and made way to the mountain which was literally right across the street from my campsite. Perfect! It was now Thanksgiving Day and most "normal" people were eating turkey in a few hours, so everyone was out early. The weather was on my side for limiting the crowds, though. It was pretty warm, in the 50s, so a lot of people just said fuck it and didn't go at all. The heat was a blessing and a curse. On one hand I was stoked to go down the mountain in just my retro black and purple Surf Styles jacket that I had gotten from the thrift store years ago. I didn't need a heavy winter coat, so my favorite windbreaker would be just fine. On the other hand it was going to be a lot of slush and ice after a few hours. It was Thanksgiving day and I was snowboarding in Lake Tahoe with clear blue skies, so it wasn't going to be much complaints out of me.

Heavenly Mountain Resort was just that, heavenly. I was heading up the first gondola and a girl said to me, "you look like Thor." For those that don't know, Thor is played by Chris Hemsworth, who by all accounts, is a ten. So this girl had basically just called me a ten. I had long hair and a beard, but other than that, the only thing that Thor and I had in common was that we both swung a big hammer. Actually, we didn't even have that in common, my hammer was average size, at best. The girl was about ten years old, so I obviously skipped telling the hammer joke out loud. Ten year olds always say what's on their mind, unfiltered and unsolicited, so hearing that I looked like an absolute stud, whether it was from a ten year old or a ninety year old, is always going to make me smile. She was a funny little girl and on Thanksgiving, without my family, talking and laughing with her and her family was just the kind of sober, innocent family fun that I needed to start my day and reduce my homesickness.

She was with her dad, her younger brother, and her grandfather. Her grandfather was an absolute legend. He knew everything about the mountain and was incredibly friendly giving me tips on which lifts to hit during the day and which bars to hit at night. People are almost always nice on a ski lift because... well, why not? People are even nicer to someone alone on a ski lift. Skiing or snowboarding with a buddy or with my old man is always better than going alone, but even when you're alone, the ski community is a friendly one, so I didn't feel alone. I hadn't even thought to look up the trail maps or anything. I was just going to take the gondola up and ride around until I found some runs I liked and stay there. This guy had not only mapped out my day, but mapped out my night too, so my day was off to a hell of a start. Who needs TripAdvisor? I had Old Man Tahoe.

I got up the gondola and took the lift he had recommended, which took me to one of the most picture perfect views I had seen in my life. You could see a massive chunk of the bluest lake, and mountains on yonder. I had boarded plenty of places in the US and in Europe, but I had never seen water and mountains like this all in one shot. The mountains were white, frosted with snow, but the lake hadn't frozen over yet. Did I mention the water was blue? When I was going down, I couldn't help but stare up at the lake instead of the trail ahead. I'm lucky I didn't slam into some skier passing by, or worse a tree, but my vision was consumed by these all time views.

I had lunch at the filling station on the mountain. Although I was too cheap to spring for the twelve dollar pizza or eighteen dollar burger that ski places always charge on the mountain with their monopoly, I wasn't cheap enough to not get myself an eight dollar brew to enjoy with my homemade turkey sando and PB&J. There is something special about a mountain beer. You're already cold, but the cold beer slithering down your throat that you can feel all the way down through your insides is even colder. I might like a cold beer on a cold mountain even more than I like a cold beer on a hot beach. And I love a cold beer on a hot beach. I could sit on that outdoor picnic table, with the sun upon my face and the blue lake popping in my eyes, sniffing the mountain air and getting a light buzz for hours. The mountain buzz is different because you're at altitude so one beer feels like two, but that's all you need. I went back out onto the mountain with a full belly and a head full of liquid confidence. It was a dangerous combo on an icy day.

At around 14:00, conditions were getting a little sketchy with the ice, and I decided to take one last run and then call it. I had gotten a solid five hours in, and it was free since I had the Epic Pass, so I was more than content with how my Thanksgiving was going. I took the last run on a blue that I had gone on a few times and enjoyed. There was a jump towards the end that I took earlier in the day and got some decent air; it was time to try it out again. I headed towards it with a full head of steam. Anchor Steam actually was the beer I drank at the bar, so it was literally a head of steam. That combo of liquid courage with the icy conditions on the jump won this battle. I slipped and landed hard on my arm.

My friends and I have a saying, "You always get hurt on the last run." Basically, that last run you're always trying to get one last trick in or one last bomb down and it usually ends with one last wipe out. When I went down, I literally thought I was going to have to go to the hospital and get my arm put into a cast. I was down for about five seconds thinking that, but it eventually subsided and by the end of the run I was completely fine with just a little soreness. I chuckled to myself, you always get hurt on the last run.

I got down the mountain in one piece, took the gondola down without any compliments from females of any age, and was ready to do the second best part of a snowboard trip, après ski! I got down the mountain and went into one of the local watering holes that Old Man Tahoe had suggested. It was right at the bottom of the gondola in the mini town on the left. I walked in and knew OMT knew what he was talking about. It was my kind of place.

There was a bar with about ten barstools and craft beers were written on a chalkboard. There were families and out of towners in their twenties, like myself, sitting at tables and a few locals just kicking it at the bar. As far as food went, the options were nachos, or fried chicken of multiple different varieties; wings, tenders, etc. It was the Thanksgiving meal I was looking for. I figured I'd hang out there for a couple hours, watch the NFL football games, drink a couple beers, eat dinner and then head to bed for an early night to get back on the mountain at first tracks tomorrow. Little did I know, a whole different kind of night was coming for me.

I took my seat at the corner of the bar with a couple of older guys a few seats down. One thing you'll learn about me from reading this, is I absolutely love going to bars alone. I don't mean that in the depressing way, like every night I hit the local saloon looking to get wasted drinking alone in the corner. I mean I love sitting at a bar, buddying up with a bartender, meeting some fine people that come in and out, paying my tab and probably never seeing those people again. It lets you be your true self because nobody has any expectations of you, so you can try out some new jokes, tell some old stories, or just simply shoot the shit with some guys about meaningless bar banter with the latter being my favorite.

I sat down and the barkeep headed down my way and first asked if I'm alone or waiting for people. I laughed and told him jokingly that, nope I was alone, just me and my family of one on this Thanksgiving, but thank you for asking. He chuckled back and grabbed me the Racer 5 I decided to order. He introduced himself as Terry; I liked this guy right away. He asked for my ID and saw I'm from Maryland, which as wild as it was, was where him and his buddy down at the end of the bar were from as well. At first exchange, we didn't have any mutual friends or connections, so the conversation kind of died down there.

The best part about solo bar-going, is people flock to you like ducks to stale Wonder Bread. They weren't flocking to me because they think I look like Thor, or any other smoke celebrity, which I didn't. They flock because whenever you see someone alone at a bar, they are approachable, and more than likely, they want to talk to someone. So people, being kind at heart as I believe them to be, want that guy alone to feel included whether they, too, are alone or they have some other buddies that could use another perspective in the conversation. The first person to sit down next to me was a milfy older lady named Sandy. With my wings polished off and the one beer — that I told Terry would be my only — getting towards the bottom, I decided to order another. Terry saw what was going on and gave me a "what do we have here?" kind of smile when he dropped off Racer 5, beer 2. She had red hair and a gentle smile, and she was recently divorced. We ended up hitting it off for about thirty minutes and at one point I swear she was making a pass at me. She was alone, too, but was meeting a friend for drinks after this one and was about to head out. She was giving me these eyes like I had only ever seen when a girl wanted to sleep with me, which I assure you was rare, so I knew it when I saw it. Then, she told me where she's staying and what bar she was going to later and that I should meet her there. She gave me the rest of her nachos and told me she's got to run. My dinner was now nachos, wings, and beer. The pilgrims would have been proud.

Before the door even closed as she walked out, my buddy Terry strolled over and said, "You never told me you were in town to pick up older ladies?! What was that, a Tinder date?!" He had clearly observed the sex eyes she was throwing at me as well.

I said, "In my defense, she was divorced and could have sat at any seat at the bar, but she chose the seat to my left." Me, him and one of the older, crusty guys sitting to my left all chalked it up for a few minutes, giggling like school boys meeting girls for the first time.

The next group to come in and talk to me was a group of guys and girls from Sacramento that were around my age. Billy sat in the seat to my left, where the older guy had been, and his buddies all filed in to the left of him. Billy was a stand up guy and he talked to me like I was one of the people in their group. In fact, he talked to me even more than he talked to most of his group. They were all good people and at one point one of them asked where I was from, I told them Maryland and Billy asks, "have you ever been to this place... uh Ocean City?" If he wanted to stay at the bar for a few hours, this was the perfect question to ask someone like me.

I told him of course I'd been there and he asked the most ignorant question you could ask someone that has been to Ocean City, "Have you ever been to Seacrets?" Again, I told him of course, but this time with some more gusto! Terry, from the other side of the bar, heard the question and chimed in that he, too, had been to heaven on earth. Seacrets is the greatest bar in America, on the bay of Ocean City, covered in sand and palm trees and with floaty rafts in the water that you can get served on. Veteran tip: don't go to the raft area. That is where everyone pees when the line for the pisser is too long. I am guilty of this as well. I want some of my ashes spread at Seacrets when I go, seriously. Billy ended up leaving and me and Terry just started to go off about Ocean City.

He asked "Did you ever live there?"

I replied, "Two summers once on Trimper and once on 75th street."

"Did you just say Trimper?"

"Yeah, you know the street?"

"You kidding? I lived there too! Franky," Terry announced to his other buddy sitting at the end of the bar, "this guy lived on Trimper!"

Franky responded with a smile, "Well... YOU didn't exactly live there."

It turned out Terry lived there in his truck. That's right, the bartender I met in Lake Tahoe, California lived in Ocean City, Maryland on the same street as me the same summer in his truck! Terry tells me not to think it's weird. He lived in the truck, but showered at buddies' places and saved cash while having the summer of his life. Terry wasn't a hobo looking guy, or a total hippy. As a matter of fact, he seemed like a total stud. At the time of his Trimper Truck Life, he was dating a smoking hot chick that was now the manager of the bar he worked at. Even though it was odd they could still work together, it was comforting to see that this cool, down to earth guy who was dating a real beauty was also a guy that lived in his truck.

This was additional proof to my original point that this movement is much more common than most people realize. There are people doing it out of want and not just people doing it out of need, and it is growing for the former with the stigma around it changing, albeit slowly. A lot more people like Terry and I were out there and we weren't the bums that people imagined when they heard, "homeless." We were just looking for more and that more for us came on the road. Terry, like the guy I saw in the 24 hour fitness parking lot, was more proof that I wasn't as crazy as some people made me feel.

Even though he lived in a house now, Terry also talked about his place down in Puerto Rico. He explained it basically as just a plot of land that he had an airstream parked on, saying, "I don't care about having a big house down there because, when I'm there, all I want to do is be outside surfing or drinking beers on my lawn. So I built out my outdoor area to look sweet, and then the airstream just has the necessities." It was more evidence that this sort of thing was not just for the hippies and hobos, but for the guys that just wanted a place to rest their heads at night in a town that they could tear up during the day. I knew I liked this guy from the start.

We shot the shit, swapping OC war stories for hours. Him and Franky mentioned this guy, Cane, a bunch of times back and forth and I never put it together. Then, he said something about Cane at Seacrets. And I tell him I had a buddy, one of my closest friends and roommates in OC, Johnny, who worked at Seacrets too.

"What did he do there?" he asked me.

"He worked on the boats that the people use to Taxi people in to Seacrets from the bay."

"Oh no way, Cane did that too."

And then it all hit me. "Wait a second. Your buddy was Captain Cane?!"

Terry and Franky lost it. They couldn't believe I knew Captain Cane. CC actually was a crucial part of one of the greatest days of my life. We were living in OC and needed a guy to be the designated driver for a boat we were going to rent for Johnny's birthday. Johnny convinced Cane to whip our dumb, drunk, freshman in college asses all around the Assawoman Bay in Ocean City. While he drove, we were doing flips off the side, shotgunning beers, and throwing cake at each other. He did all this in exchange for just a case of beer and not paying for the boat, obviously. The whole time everyone was loving Captain Cane and he was the perfect driver on one of the best days of my life. I am forever indebted to him, and to meet some of his best friends all the way across the country all these years later was too good to be true.

After my Thanksgiving dinner, Sandy and Billy's coming and going, OC stories swapped, and the one beer I was supposed to have that turned into six because I was having such a blast, it was time for the bar to close. It was Thanksgiving, after all. Everyone trickled out except for me and Franky. Other people were walking in, but Terry was telling them it's closed and they couldn't come in. I started to get my hat and coat on and got ready to head out, but Terry told me I didn't have to leave. He had to close down anyways so he said he didn't mind me and Franky kicking it with him, but nobody else was allowed to stay or enter. In four hours, I felt like I had earned regular status, the best status one could earn at a bar in my opinion.

We closed out and I thought I was really done with my beers and ready to pass out, when Terry whips out a bottle of whiskey and poured three shots for the three Ocean City boys in Tahoe, free of charge. Even after that, when I thought I was ready to roll out, Franky goes behind the bar and looks at Terry with a tilted head and a face like, "cool if I pour my own beer?" Terry made a kind of stink face and nodded as if to say, "of course, what are you even asking me for?" Then, to top the night off, and supplant me feeling even more like a regular at a bar I had never been, Terry said, "Petey, get on back here too and pour yourself another one." In all my life I had never felt more accepted in a place that I didn't initially belong than how I felt pouring that draft beer out of the tap into my glass as if I was the owner of the bar. Just like Junger said, humans want to feel a part of a group. Today, on my first Thanksgiving away from my family, this group was everything I could ask for. We hit one more bar together and called it a night. I never saw Terry or Franky again, but you better believe if I ever head up to Tahoe again, that is the first bar I am stopping at. Hopefully when the night is through, I am again pouring my own pints sharing laughs with some strangers that turned into best friends for a night.

Many of the greatest moments I had over my time travelling were in interactions like this. My time alone had taught me to engage more with strangers and be more comfortable in my own skin to do so. I was able to live more in the moment, because I was doing so more often. Instead of getting to the bar and sitting on my phone the whole time, I was looking for these types of interactions, and they came to me.

Powell Berger, one of the vagabonds in Rolf Potts's *Vagabonding*, put what I was thinking perfectly into words. She said, "We put so many barriers between ourselves and human interaction" (Potts, p. 140)[11], or basically that we find any excuse not to go out of our way to interact with other people. Travelers have long talked about how important it is to get to know the people you meet when you travel rather than to be wrapped up in your own little bubble or sucked into your phone so that you don't have to ask directions from anyone. Old Man Tahoe, who knew the mountain best, told me where to snowboard and where to get my pints afterwards. All of his tips proved to be spot on, and all of the people that I met at the bar, whether they were travelers like me or people that lived in Tahoe, were delightful. Terry showed me to another bar that was also a blast and he didn't have to do that, and he wouldn't have if I was the snobby millennial that just sat at the bar on my phone not talking to anyone, or if I had just gone back to the truck at the end of the day of snowboarding and gone straight to bed. This idea of getting out and experiencing more was one of the top reasons that I wanted to live in the truck and now it was proving to be worthwhile.

I woke up the next morning a little hungover, but mostly content and rolled out of the truck to start the whole routine from yesterday over again. The next day wasn't as eventful. The conditions were a little worse as the heat from the day before had melted some of the snow and then refroze it over night leading to icy and slushy conditions. I got in another half a day and decided to call it before I got hurt on another last run. It was only about one full day of snowboarding in total when you added it all up, but it was a hell of a snowboard trip.

I left town around 14:00 after checking out the beach at Lake Tahoe and grabbing some lunch. It was time to drive from Tahoe to Santa Barbara. The drive was nice for the first bit, as I passed the incredible surrounding towns of Tahoe with waterfalls along the side of the highways and long views of the horizon. About halfway there, I stopped at a rest station for dinner. PB&J was on the menu once again and the rest station turned out to have some pretty decent views.

By the time it got dark, I was getting more and more tired. I had gotten a shitty night of sleep before with all of those beers in me and the late night with my new travel buddies. Add a half day of going up and down the mountain and it equaled a wiped out version of myself. I resorted to the eyes wide open out the window with music blasting technique to keep myself awake again and around 22:00, I pulled into Santa Barbara.

A buddy of mine had lived there in college and told me where to park if I wanted to car camp. It was in the college part of town during Thanksgiving break, so I assumed it would be pretty relaxed in terms of anyone caring about seeing me sleeping in there. I drove around for a little bit looking for a quiet street and finally found a spot under some trees with a few houses around in case of an emergency, but not enough houses around to be seen. The streetlamps were dimly lit so I didn't feel like I was in a sketchy part of town, but also wasn't blinded by the light.

When I got back into the truck, I was ready to pass out. There was a party going on a little bit down the way that I could hear remnants of. It was quiet enough for me to be able to fall asleep, but loud enough for me to know that it was a party and to miss the college days. I fell asleep with ease and was ready to get after it in the morning.

My buddy had suggested I park here because it was near two of the best surf breaks in town. When I woke up, I moved my truck closer to the path that I would need to take to get down to the break. It was a dirt path, but on either side of the dirt path, was just more brown, dead grass. To my left was the horizon of the ocean and to my right was tall trees, and not palm trees like I was used to seeing in surf areas. These were just normal trees that made me feel like there was no way that I could be this close to the ocean. I walked down the path to check out the two spots and decide which one I wanted to go to. The coastline jetted out into sea to a point with coves for surfbreaks on both sides. To the left was a place called Devereux and to the right was Sands. I walked out to the point looked at both breaks and decided that I was going to hit Sands.

The recommendation also came with a warning. He told me that if I saw black stuff on the beach or got some on my foot, not to worry, this was just part of the lay of the land. I guess a little bit of oil had washed up on to shore and every now and then, you could step on a spot of it and get some oil stuck to your foot. Luckily, I'd be wearing booties, so I didn't have much to worry about.

I followed the trail back to my truck to grab my board and walked back down the path, past the point, and down the hill to get to the beach. I paddled out there, careful to be respectful to the locals, without any oil stuck to me and surfed for a few hours before my balls couldn't take the cold anymore. It was a much different break than what I was used to in San Diego, so it was a blast. The air was colder, the waves broke differently, and there were a lot less people, so I had more room to operate and more opportunities to catch waves without cutting anyone off. I walked back up to the point stood out there, breathing in the fattest sniff of ocean air I could get and was ready to make the trip home.

I got some lunch at a burrito place my friend had recommended and then made the five hour trip back from Santa Barbara to San Diego. I was excited to get back and see my friends, maybe even grab some beers on that Saturday night if I made decent time, but I couldn't stop thinking about the trip as I journeyed back. The waves were cold, the slopes were warm, but the unusual Thanksgiving was one better than I had ever pictured and one I'd never forget.

9

DAYS LIKE THIS

(2:06)

A lot of this story revolves around my favorites trips and what I gained from those experiences because frankly, those tend to sum up the time in my truck best. Traveling was also one of the main reasons that I wanted to do it, so I felt like writing about those trips were most important to include as the majority of this book, but I'd be remiss not to just talk about my regular old day to day life. This chapter will try to do that.

The truth is, my life was pretty normal minus the hopping in and out of bed, which I think I have spoken about enough in detail. Everything else was just me trying to live my best life, showering at a gym, doing laundry at the launromat, and peeing and pooping in public restrooms. When people ask what was different about it, that's basically the short version answer.

My day began promptly at 05:27 every morning with the sound of my iPhone alarm echoing in my cave of a bedroom, waking me up with the thought that I was excited to be up and to have made it through another solid night of sleep of rent free living without a problem. I was always ready to get out of bed because I wanted to not stir around too much in case anyone heard my alarm and was waiting for me to get out.

So, I'd put my pants on that I had rested by the foot of my bed, wiggling to get them on in a delicate balance of not using too much energy and keeping my head low to not hit my head on the ceiling, an art I had mastered after about a month. My wallet and keys were on the shelf on the port side of my room, the opposite side of where my head rested when I slept. I'd lift up my mattress pad on the starboard side of my truck and reach into the compartment between where my drawers ended and my truck bed wall began. This is where I'd store my slides every night, the ones I would wear into the gym and then shower in. I'd slip those on, slip off the locks to my hatch, peep around to see if anyone was walking their dog or up at this hour walking around for any reason, kick the hatch open, and hop out.

The time was now probably 05:31. I'd get to the front of my truck and hop into the cab. From my usual sleeping spots, it was about a twenty minute drive to the gym. Once I got to the gym parking lot, I was basically in my own walk in closet getting ready. I'd park towards the back of the lot to not cause a big scene. It was an underground lot at six in the morning, so there weren't a lot of people rolling by. I didn't want to disrupt people going to the gym, having them think I was one of those crazy homeless people that they had to avoid, so I always parked further away from the rest of the cars than I needed to.

Once I was parked, I could grab my backpack from the cab. After a few months, the backpack was pretty much the only thing in the cab that I had laying around. I started the journey with a cooler and a plastic container with drawers. I ended up taking out only the shit I needed from the plastic drawers and putting those in any storage pocket of my truck available. I took the cooler out and only used it for trips since I was eating all of my dinners and weekend meals out, and my breakfasts and lunches at work. The only food and drink I kept in the truck were the protein bars in the glove box that I would eat on the way to the gym and water bottles that I would keep in my cup holder. The rest either was thrown out, donated, or moved to the storage unit. I was Marie Kondo before Marie Kondo was cool.

With the backpack in hand, I'd walk around to the back. Then, I'd pop open the hatch, pull down the tailgate and usually close the hatch again so that I could just see the drawers and pull them out, but nobody could see into the mattress section of the truck bed. From here, I'd grab my stinky sneakers from my dirty clothes drawer, my other gym clothes (if I wasn't already wearing them as pajamas), and what I would wear for work that day and put them all in the backpack. Also already in the backpack were my toiletries, comb, etc. It had everything I needed to get ready for the day after my workout. I'd walk into the gym and say hello to Mary at the front desk. She was a big sweetheart and always a welcoming first person to see every morning. Since I hadn't peed since the night before, I'd hustle into the locker room and pee before doing anything else. It was usually one of those pees where you have to go so bad that it feels like you are releasing every piece of tension from your body. Once I peed, I'd lock up everything in one of the gym lockers and head out.

My workout would usually begin with shooting some hoops, something I loved doing, but didn't do nearly enough when I wasn't going to the gym as much. Once I was warmed up, I'd go hit the weights. I'd finish the workout, grab a towel, grab my conditioner and shampoo from my locker (body wash included with the gym membership, what a steal!), and hit the shower. Once I got out, I'd get dressed into my work clothes, comb my hair, and brush my teeth in the gym bathroom. Most of the guys that went to the gym in the early morning did all of this, too, so I didn't stick out from anyone.

Once I left the gym, I'd get to the truck, put my dirties in the dirty clothes drawer with my gym shoes, and change from my slides into my work shoes. Then, I'd close up the shell. From here, I'd finish the remaining ten minutes of my commute to work. The gym was right along the way, so it just broke up the commute. It helped me miss most of the traffic every morning because the last ten minutes were never crowded, but the first twenty could be thirty or forty if I went later in the morning and skipped the gym. When I got to work, I'd get out my protein powder and tub of oatmeal, both of which I kept in a drawer at my desk. People usually ask how I ate — so boom — there's one meal. Oatmeal with honey and a protein shake was breakfast every Monday through Friday. Saturdays and Sunday I would treat myself to a breakfast out. Pancakes were my favorite, so I usually ate those once a week.

There was nothing else that was different about my work day than a usual work day. Kenny, my good friend living in San Diego, told his sister in-law and my coworker, Megan, about my living situation. Megan and my friend Emily were the only people at the office who knew. I didn't want anybody to think of me any differently or think that I was short on money, so I just kept it to myself. I met Megan's mom when she came into town and she had found out about my truck living. When she got home she asked Megan how I did it. Kenny was there, so he told me Megan had said, "You'd have zero clue that he lived in his truck just by working with him." I was a polite, respectful kid, a hard worker, didn't smell like a foot, and kept myself well groomed, all things you would not expect from one of us homeless folk, so nobody suspected a thing. In fact, one time my team had even had a long conversation about the people living in RVs, or living in cars at Wal-Marts. It got brought up because there was a guy living in his RV on the street outside of our office. The whole team was kind of making fun of those people and making us out to all be crazy or complete hippies. Little did they know, we could be a lot more like them than they thought. One of those crazy people was right in their midst.

After work was where I found the routine between truck and house life to be the most different. I'd head out from work, throw on the *Pardon the Interruption* podcast to get my sports fix without having to watch TV and drive towards the beach town I loved. The rest of the day was usually:

Do something outside until it got dark

Eat dinner

Find somewhere to read or relax

Go to bed

Let's start with the doing something until it got dark. There was almost never a night that I missed the sunset. I had no reason not to; I loved spending time outside, and I had nowhere else to be, so it was an excellent combination. I'd usually surf if the waves were halfway decent. If they weren't I'd read at the beach or ride my bike along the boardwalk.

I found so many little things that made me smile out there in the time between the end of the work day and the end of the daylight. There was one time when I surfed with a famous singer just by chance. He was paddling out with me and a few of the other guys recognized him and started chatting him up. It wasn't my type of music, so I didn't really know who he was until later, but it was still cool to be out there with him and he seemed like a down to earth guy. Whether it was experiencing something like that, people watching on the boardwalk, or playing volleyball with friends, I grew to appreciate the people around me a lot more and appreciate the alone time I had as well.

One of my favorite experiences, though, was one night I was watching the sunset out on my favorite cliff. There were a few houses by the north side of the cliff and most people sat on the south side to watch it, but for whatever reason, I was sitting on the north side on this night, watching a cotton candy sky fade to night, with my skin still crusty from the salt of the ocean. I watched as a man approached from his house carrying a cardboard box and another piece of cardboard. I know he didn't see me as I was off to the side and he looked too focused on what he was doing. He walked towards the front of the cliff, put the box down and put up a sign in front of the box. He walked away with this little content grin, the kind of grin that says that all is right with your own world and the world is all right with you. I was especially curious as to what this box and sign could possibly be, so I checked it out.

As I got closer I saw that the sign said "FREE", and in the box were freshly picked oranges. I assumed that these were from his own orange tree in his backyard, they looked too natural to be from a store. It still gives me goosebumps thinking about that grin that this man had on his face. He was giving people free oranges because it made him feel good and he didn't need anyone to see that he was doing it or make a big stink to tell everyone that they could have some of *his* free oranges. He was just happy for the doing. And the doing, without anyone else's approval or gratitude, gave me more joy and more clarity than any little act of kindness I had ever witnessed. It felt like the metaphor for me living in my truck. As long as I was doing what I enjoyed, trying to find ways to give myself that little grin, that was what it was all about. It didn't matter if people did or did not see that I was happy, it mattered that I knew it, just as my man knew that those oranges would be enjoyed without anyone telling him. Seeing moments like this, on days where if I was living in a house I probably would have never been there for, made me more and more grateful.

Once the sun set, and the oranges were grabbed (of course I grabbed one), I'd go out to eat dinner. Usually I'd take my book with me and read a few pages while I waited and sometimes after I ate. Since I was saving so much money living rent-free, the extra money to eat out didn't make me feel guilty and also allowed me to try places that I never had before. Some places sucked balls and I was able to tell people where to avoid at all costs, but I also found some new places that I loved.

I've always been team "eat there" rather than team "grab and go." Why anyone would want to get the food and then bring it home and eat it, when it is not the freshest, is beyond me. I love getting the food and eating at the restaurant, whether it was just me or if I was grubbing with some buddies. I'd been that way my whole life, so eating dinner out alone wasn't a big change for me; it was just much more frequent. From time to time, I'd go to a little pub and grab a bite sitting at the bar alone, something I've mentioned a few times as one of my favorite things. I loved this part of the night because dinner never felt rushed and I never felt impatient when waiting for my food. I was relaxing there, same as I would be anywhere else, so I was content.

Once dinner was done, there was one to two hours between then and when it was time to hit the sack, or beddy time as we liked to call it to MC's puppy, Brooklyn. This part of the day had become much more enjoyable than that first week. It took me a little while to get into the swing of things, but after a few months, this became one of the better parts of my day. This was where I would usually find a quiet place to read or go do yoga. During the winter months I did a lot more yoga because there was a lot more time between sunset and bed, so a lot less time to be fucking around outside. I loved it, but I am not by any means the expert and my third eye is probably blind compared to the people that should be talking to you about this kind of stuff. I'll leave the science of it all to them and just say, yeah, I enjoyed yoga and it slowed my mind.

If I wasn't doing yoga, I went to boxing classes, dance classes, caught a mid week movie or played a round of putt putt with friends amongst other things. I became a big yes man, like I had been when I lived at the beach in the summers of 2012 and 2013. Some of the stuff I did on my own, like the boxing classes. It was always something that I wanted to do, but always found a reason to delay. Now, it was the time to do it. When I had nothing else to do, I had no reason not to give these new skills a try. Other activities, I'd be a yes man with buddies. If a friend wanted to go rock climbing, I'd be up for it although I had never gone and didn't know if I'd like it. Climbing turned out to be a lot of fun, even though my forearms burned for days. I even learned how to sail one weekend with Chof. Sailing was always a dream of mine and turned out to be more special than I'd ever imagined. To me, this was what it was all about — getting more out of life by getting out and living it.

The effects of exercise on happiness have been acknowledged for a long time and it is well known that getting in a sweat consistently can make someone significantly happier. My long bike rides, boxing classes, going to the gym, and other athletic experiences were definitely making me happier, but I won't bore you with those details since those effects are

116

obvious. However, the same is also true for experiences outside of athletic activities. Studies have shown that people are happier with spending their money on experiences than on material things (Kumar, Killingsworth & Gilovich, 2014).[12] Since I was living in my truck, and didn't really have any room or desire to buy material shit, almost all of my spending (outside of gas and necessities) were going towards experiences. Instead of buying that new TV, I was buying tickets to a ball game or a Groupon to learn a new hobby. I feel like the idea that people are happier doing than having is especially true for millenials like me. I am constantly finding that the best gifts my friends are buying for their significant others are the trips or concert tickets rather than the new bag or watch.

The thing that I probably did most often was grab a book and walk down to this hotel with a wide open bayfront area. The beach was open to the public, and I wasn't bugging anyone, so I would go and find a palm tree to sit under. The trees had lights above them and fake turf underneath them, which made it a comfortable place to sit on that didn't even require me to bring my booklight. Some nights they'd have movies on a massive inflatable screen on the sand. I'd be lying if I said I didn't decide to forget about the book one night and watch *Cars 3* out there, instead. On Wednesdays and Thursdays, there would be a guy playing acoustic and singing classics, which to me was like heaven.

I'd have to say that this was my favorite thing to do at nights during my time living in the truck. That same study I mentioned in earlier on about the correlation of television watching and happiness, talked about how they found that the happier people engaged in social activities and read more (Robinson & Martin).[8] I was still spending a ton of time with friends, which was great, but when I wasn't, the books I read kept me engaged and relaxed with the world around me. I was getting something out of every book I read, whether it was just one line I'd carry with me or a whole mindset that the author was detailing. On the contrary, I never really got anything from watching a random sports game (aside from the teams that I root for), which is what I was doing a lot of in my house life. I wouldn't think about the Spurs vs. Lakers game in January that I was watching just to pass the time ever again once it ended. The way that I value a book is how much I think about it afterwards and many of those books that I read have stuck with me in the months and years since.

One night with the sound of little waves lapping up against the shore and Tom Petty's "Wildflowers" being covered by the local talent for the night, I sat under my usual tree and flipped through some pages. It was a crisp spring night, where a sweatshirt and boardshorts was the perfect outfit. The sky was clear and the night was shaping up to be absolutely delightful when a little kid walked up to me. He had been playing frisbee with his sister in the grassy area by the beach and after an errant throw by her, he ended up plopped next to me.

"That's a beautiful place to wead," he said with a slight speech impediment, but with palpable confidence.

"Yes, yes it is, it's a beautiful place to do just about anything huh?" I responded.

"What are you weadin'?" the little fella asked.

"It's a book called *Abundance*" I told him, referring to the Peter Diamandis book about people, much smarter than me, fixing the world's biggest problems. It was a book that was a little complex for my pea brain, so I didn't expect my new little buddy to relate to the book at all or have an open forum on the writing style of Diamandis.

He looked at me with wide eyes and that interested, eyebrow raised, frown that little kids do and nodded. It was the type of nod as if *Abundance* was the next book on his nightstand, too. "Oh cool!" he said and then darted off to keep playing his game of frisbee. Months later as I jot this down, it still makes me smile thinking of that spot and that interaction because a beautiful place to wead it was.

Once the night crept toward bedtime, I'd walk to whereever I was parked, peeing in a public bathroom somewhere along the way. This was always crucial because, if not, I'd wake up in the middle of the night and not have the luxury of my own pisser to use. I was never a go in the middle of the night kind of guy. I hated the feeling of cold tile on barefeet in the middle of the night, so I would usually tough it out until the morning, even when I lived in a house. While living in my truck, I was even less of a pee in the middle of the night guy as it required me to leave my house. As I described from my first night, this was not a desirable option.

When I made it back to the truck, I would get in the driver's seat. I'd grab my backpack from the backseat and get out the toiletry bag. Then, I would take my contacts out and brush my teeth, using a splash of water from a water bottle. I always had a water bottle on hand in my front seat cup holder for splashes like this and random sips. I always felt weird spitting the toothpaste spit outside because I felt like this was the worst dead giveaway. If I ever saw someone see me doing it, usually I'd just move somewhere else to sleep for the night since there was no sense in risking it. Once that was all said and done, it was time to unlock the hatch and call it a night.

The thing about the sleeping aspect of the truck that surprised me was the fact that I was actually sleeping better than when I lived in a house. I didn't have as comfortable of a bed and as I mentioned earlier, it was not as large of a bed. I was sleeping diagonally to fit on it and I had little room above my head for me to feel comfortable. So, no, I was not sleeping better because of the actual bed. Most of the things that I was doing to sleep better, I can take with me after I move out of the truck and plan to do so. After that first week or so, when I was so stressed out and new to the whole thing, I was able to relax when I got into bed because of a lot of sleep clichés that turned out to be true.

The first and the most important change in my mind was the one that you always hear growing up from your mother. "Don't watch TV before you go to bed, you're gonna be up all night!" That, along with the mindless scrolling on the phone, would hurt my sleep for a long time, but in the truck I wasn't doing that. The TV part was easy, seeing as I didn't have a Dish or DirecTV hooked up to my wheel estate, but the phone part was pretty easy too. I didn't want to draw a lot of attention to myself, so I didn't want that light to be shining in my truck bed illuminating the whole thing inside and out. As a result, I pretty much never used my phone in bed. It also helped that in place of those binge TV sessions, I was usually reading before bed, another cliché that proved to be true for me with helping my REM cycle.

We move from advice from the mother to advice from the grandmother. Chof's grandmother always told him that you should sleep with a window open because the fresh air will help you breathe easier and keep you from getting sick. I have no idea if this is scientifically true, but Chof's grandmother is a saint, so who am I to argue with that? Also, I never once got sick while living in the truck. I'm not saying, "Live in a truck, you'll have a perfect immune system!" But, that's the truth, so maybe the fresh air really did keep me from being sick. I usually parked with the opened window by my head facing the ocean. This way, the cool ocean draft went in through there and out the side windows for some nice cross-breeze. I was able to keep warm, but never really got overheated.

There was one time when sleeping with the window open came back to fuck me, though. It was around month two when I woke up from a dead sleep to a fluttering sound echoing throughout my shell. I couldn't see a goddamn thing, so I grabbed my iPhone and shined the flashlight around. Sure enough, this massive moth was cruising around my house like it was a damn zoo. I was swatting at it every which way to try to get it out, banging around in the back of the pickup making it rock all around. If someone was up at this hour and saw the illuminated truck bed making this motion, they'd surely think that some college kids were bumping boots back there, but that was far from the truth. To be honest, I was surprised this didn't happen more often, but thank god it didn't. That was the first and only bug scare.

Another key ingredient to a decent night's sleep was darkness, obviously. I read that they did studies where they would shine lights on the back of people's knees and their bodies could still detect that light. In order for you to get the best possible sleep, it needs to be pitch black, so that as little light as possible could be detected (Ferriss, p. 126).[13] The shell was dark to begin with, but to start getting the best sleep, I had to get really dark with it. I ended up taking the tapestry out and replacing it with black curtains. The tapestry gave it a homey touch, but also was a pain in the ass. Since it was all connected, if you bumped one part of it down, it was likely that other parts were coming down. In the middle of the night in an already claustrophobic setting, a massive cloth falling down over your face wasn't ideal. So, I got blackout curtains. One for each wall to cover up each window, not attached to each other. I kept them up with safety pins, which was a huge improvement from that dumbass decision to use Velcro to hang the tapestry, piercing them into the curtain and then into the carpeted roof of the camper shell. When those things were hung, I couldn't see my hand if it was right in front of my face when it was night time. All of the rumors were true: Darkness was key for an elite night of sleep.

The last cliché that I'll bore you with is that your bed should only be for sleep. Well, the saying usually goes that your bed should only be for sleep and sex... but let's be honest, given the circumstances. If those situations were to miraculously happen, I was ideally not bringing her home; I was sleeping away. Anyways, by using your bed only for sleep and the other thing, it lets you know that when you get in there, it's beddy time. I literally was never ever laying on that bed unless I was trying to sleep, so after a while, it was easy for that brain of mine to realize that the time for fucking around was over and it was now time for sleep. It really worked. It was taking me less and less time to fall asleep, which was something I had struggled with for basically my whole life.

It wasn't all sunshine and rainbows with the sleeping, though. When it rained, it could get a little loud with the raindrops banging on the metal roof eighteen inches above my head. Lucky for me, it almost never rained in San Diego. Even if I absolutely needed to, I knew I had a strong support network and could sleep at a friend's if needed. Sammy and David, a lovely couple that I had only met a couple handful of times through Banks's Dad, offered me their guest room anytime I needed it. It was unbelievably sweet of them, but really I was fine. There was also the issue of the drunk nights of sleep. On nights when I had a few too many beers, I dreaded hitting the Tacoma Hay for a few reasons. One, I knew I would have to pee in the middle of the night. You know the type of hungover pee where you feel like your stomach is going to explode? I had that every time I slept in Taco drunk. Two, there is no worse feeling than waking up in a cramped spot hungover. Again, lucky for me, I had amazing pals, and if I had indeed had a few too many, I could crash on their couch. Unlike Sammy and David's offer, I cashed in on that offer a couple of times.

At the end of the day, the standard night, no beers, no rain, was a solid night of sleep. I had much fewer nights of tossing and turning and woke up in the middle of the night less frequently. The white noise of the cars whooshing by didn't even phase me after a while. Like I said earlier, it wasn't the actual truck or the bed that was helping me do all of this, but the healthy habits that I was forming. Either way, I was just happy to be getting enough winks to feel lively enough to wake up in the morning, hit the gym, and do it all over again.

10

NO SURRENDER

(2:33)

My boss said I was free to go at 14:15 and, before he could finish his sentence, my monitors were off and I was packing my shit to leave. It was the Friday of Memorial Day weekend, and I needed to take advantage of the day off and get out there. I hadn't taken an extended trip in Taco since Tahoe really so this was a long overdue road trip.

Since I had moved to California, Big Sur was one of my top destinations I knew I had to explore, right up there with Joshua Tree. Since it was an eight hour drive without MDW traffic and I was leaving straight from work, I figured it would be best to break it up and stop somewhere first so that I wasn't driving through Big Sur in the pitch black of night. I settled on a place called Pismo Beach. It was supposed to have a sweet shore break and a nice little beach town vibe, so it sounded like the perfect pit stop to me.

On the Monday of MDW, my buddy Sock was going to be in Half Moon Bay. He won a stay at the Ritz-Carlton through work and was planning on going alone. Naturally, since I was going to be only a couple hours south of that, I asked if he'd mind if I tagged along and played golf with him. To which he responded, "yeah I don't care I'm gonna be bored as fuck alone." The final piece to the puzzle was asking my boss to work remotely on the Tuesday. I freaked out about asking but finally when I did he said, "yeah I don't care." That seemed to be a theme for the weekend.

Amazingly, something came up where I needed to work in our Los Angeles distribution center on Wednesday. It couldn't have worked out better because now I could spend all day in Half Moon Bay Tuesday, drive half way to SoCal Tuesday night and sleep in the same spot in Santa Barbara that I slept for Thanksgiving, drive to LA Wednesday morning, get my work done and drive the rest of the way Wednesday night. My Memorial Day weekend turned into a five day vacation; I was absolutely stoked.

The drive was long and there was heavy traffic, but it really wasn't too bad. I took the 1 and the 101 for a lot of it and, man, that is a lovely drive. You've got hills and beaches, and it was timed perfectly for a prime beach sunset.

I only stopped for dinner when there was about five minutes left in the Celtics game so that I could catch the end. The burger was from this little local watering hole in Santa Barbara. It might as well have been a Burger King burger. I don't mean that in the sense that it was char broiled or whoppingly big, or whatever marketing angle the King is taking these days. I mean it had a shit ton of mustard and it tasted like buttcheeks. I liked the vibe of the place, though, so I'm not going to smear its name in this piece of literature. It reminded me of my favorite spot in San Diego, so although the burger was sub par, I wasn't mad I stopped there.

I pulled into Grover Beach right around 21:30 which was perfect for bed time. It was unknown territory for me, so finding a spot proved a little bit difficult. Every road had real homes with only a couple of cars parked on the street and every other car parked in the driveway. In San Diego, there were plenty of cars on the road, so one more didn't seem conspicuous and didn't seem like it should bother anyone. But this place seemed like my own hometown in Maryland where, if someone parked in my court with tags from a different state and didn't look like they were staying with anyone, my parents and my neighbors would probably call the police on the car. At the very least, they'd get the neighborhood watch on the case. My truck was also packed with my surfboard, golf clubs, and Sock's golf clubs, so if anyone saw this thing on the street, it'd stick out like a sore thumb.

It took me about 15 minutes, but finally I found this road with a park on one side and homes on the other. I pulled up behind another car that was parked on the park side and peeped around to see if anyone was giving me the Grover Beach Hairy Eyeball (stink eye). Once I saw the coast was clear, I did my same army crawl hop into the truck that I've done hundreds of times in San Diego. The night went off without a hitch, and I woke up at 06:30 ready to charge the waves, another town added to the list for my little home on wheels.

I had read that Pismo Beach Pier was the spot for the best waves in this town, so I got there around 06:45. I got out and looked before I put on my wetsuit and was cheesing ear to ear. It was a beautiful left. A left is when you're in the water, facing the shore and wave breaks from left to right. For a goofy surfer like me, this was ideal, seeing as I was much better facing the wave than with my backside to it. It looked like it was breaking pretty cleanly with good size and it didn't look like a Six Flags water park with dots of people filling every spot of the water like you'd see in San Diego with those same conditions. In other words, everything was lining up well.

When I was getting my wetsuit and booties in the parking lot, I noticed a ton of locals also wearing the head covers. I knew it was going to be cold, but for end of May, I didn't expect head cover cold. Fortunately, I just got a brand new 4/3 wetsuit because my old one, the one with holes and a see through area where my tallywacker is, would have given me permanent shrinkage in these cold, cold northern California waters.

I started to paddle out and my hands were frigid, but the rest of my body was a prime temperature thanks to the new suit. Even duck diving, the cold water felt refreshing on my head because the rest of my body was so cozy. I got the wetsuit in May because that's when people usually need it least so they're least expensive. Luckily for me, it was when I needed it most.

The spot I wanted to paddle out was just north of the pier, where it was breaking absolutely perfectly left. It was obviously where the most people were and, of course, where the locals were. This whole place seemed like it was filled with locals and I might very well have been the only one from out of town in the lineup. It was the kind of place where everyone shows up with a coffee mug, not a paper coffee cup. Dillon describes this as the ultimate local beach bum move. I agreed with that sentiment, but didn't exactly understand why when he first told me. It wasn't until weeks later when he texted me, "My dumb ass just figured out why it's the ultimate beach bum move. Cuz you're telling everyone you're a local. Like yeah I live here at the beach where else did I get this goddamn Barbara Bush mug?!"

I decided against paddling out with the locals in the best spot to show a little respect and also not get my tush kicked in. I went a little north and had a great session. A lot of sweet lefts and even a couple of decent rights by my awful backside standards. It was the perfect way to kick off my road trip and I was in a phenomenal mood.

After I rinsed off and changed into normal clothes, I went to a little coffee shop called Red Bee to grab a cup of joe (I probably don't need to mention I ordered it in one of their Red Bee coffee mugs rather than a paper cup) and a cwassaunt. I know it's spelled croissant, but if you're not pronouncing it in your best French accent, you might as well not even order one and go home.

Buzzing from my first cup in a month or so, I was ready for the next adventure: ATVing on the beach. I went into the reservation office and rented the cheapest ATV they had for two hours and made my way to the dunes where I was to pick her up.

The dunes were literally on the beach. You could ride along the shore or pull off further inland and tear through these massive sand dunes, all while the beautiful Pacific is a couple hundred yards to the west.

I get to the helmet pickup and the woman with braces that was working the station asks me each of the following questions with a "no" from me in between. "Are you alone? Have you ever ridden on one of these? Do you know anyone out there?" This woman was clearly concerned about me, but not enough to give me any real helpful pointers. Instead opting for basically saying, "well if you get fucked out there, the numbers on that form there," in a little country twang accent.

The next guy that gave me my bike asked me the same things, but gave me a little more instruction on how to switch gears and all that, but again, no real guidance. It was my first time on this thing, or anything like it, but I didn't care and I was pumped. This looked like it was going to be a blast.

There was an initial slow area you drove through past a bunch of campsites on the beach and then it expanded to a seemingly boundless open area with massive peaks and valleys. Once I got out there, I started to take it slow, but more and more started opening it up. You'd haul ass up the peaks and then have to loosen your grip on the accelerator in preparation for a big drop off. That was one of the very few tips I got out there, be ready for those drop offs so you don't drive yourself off of a cliff.

Once or twice I'd be too much of a pussy and slow down before I got to the peaks and get stuck. Lifting that heavy ATV out of the sand wasn't fun, but it only made the thrill of the rest of the ride more enjoyable. You know if you fuck up and get stuck, you're pulling at least one muscle in your back, so you might as well just fully send it.

I hadn't had that much fun by myself, outside of being in the water, in months. When it was all done, hands shaking from gripping the throttle and shins stinging from getting whipped with the sand shooting out from the tires, I was wiped and stoked all at once. I put my helmet down at the same place I picked it up. Jane, the helmet woman, was cheesing ear to ear when she saw my wild helmet hair and inexperienced ass made it back in one piece. I threw her a wink and went on my way to the shuttle.

The shuttle guy picked me up to take me back to town and, like everyone else at the company, asked, "are we waiting for the rest of your crew?" I laughed and said, "no sir, party of one." He was super apologetic, and felt bad, like in *Forgetting Sarah Marshall* when Jonah Hill asks Jason Segel if his wife would be joining him. He was impressed I'd go out there all alone and fly around in the vast course like a psycho without any riding experience or anyone to help if something goes wrong, but I could tell he definitely felt sympathetic thinking that I had no friends. I told him not to worry, that I was just happy to hit those jumps alone without anyone there to see me with my tail between my legs pulling the bike out of the sand later on. At this point, I never found it weird to be alone on my adventures. In fact, I wore it like a badge of honor.

Right before I decided to move into the truck, I was reading *This is Where I Leave You* on a recommendation from a friend. In it was one of my favorite quotes that I wrote down in my journal and would go back and read every so often. The main character's wife had left him and he was in a huge rut when another woman told him, "You're terrified of being alone. Anything you do now will be motivated by that fear. You have to stop worrying about finding love again. It will come when it comes. Get comfortable with being alone. It will empower you" (Tropper, p. 293).[14] I'd found that to be true. The more time I spent alone, the more comfortable I got and the less I worried about being alone. It was absolutely empowering.

I got back into town and fired up the Tahoma, primed for the next leg of the trip. Two more hours to Big Sur and if I got there early enough, I'd have time to get a solid camping spot and maybe take a hike before sunset. I popped open a Refreshe seltzer water and hit the road. I had to go inland a little bit from Grover Beach to get to Big Sur, or at least to get to the campsite that I was going to. So this meant my usual coastline drive was going to be turned into a forest drive.

My campsite was called Prewitt Ridge Campground. It was on one of those "Free Campsite" websites, but since it was Memorial Day weekend, I was worried that all of the spots were going to be taken. That worry quickly dissipated when I began making the trek. The entire way up was just steep inclines with little dips in between. It honestly felt like I was on the ATV again going up and down the dunes. The only difference was the dunes didn't have these massive cliffs next to them. And it was probably a bad thing that I had gotten some confidence that morning on the ATV and maybe hit some of those inclines a little too hard with my actual vehicle, and also my home…

When I was making the haul up, I stopped worrying about getting up there and having no camping spot. My worry now became just getting up there in one piece before night fell. I printed out the Google Maps page, a huge old timer move, but it proved to be essential because there wasn't a sniff of service up there, so I probably would have never made it up without my granny essentials. To be honest, even though the ride had its frightening points, it was a hell of a time. I had never really felt like I was off roading in my truck like I had imagined when I bought it, or how it is always portrayed in Pacifico commercials, but I had finally gotten it. A few scrapes to the truck later, I finally saw it: my campsite.

It was a little bit crowded, but I was able to find a prime spot. It was the spot that I had dreamed of when thinking about Big Sur. I was able to back my truck in so that the shell was facing the ocean. I was going to be able to wake up tomorrow, pop the door up and see Big Blue first thing. All my anxiety about finding a spot was for naught because I had found the most peaceful sleeping place that Tahoma and I would ever have.

The campsite was at the top of the ridge, so basically if you were looking down you could see over all of the clouds and through some spots you could see the ocean. I was hoping that it would be perfectly clear so that I'd just see a wall of blue, but being above the clouds was pretty sick too, so I couldn't complain. It was like you were standing on top of a hill with these massive trees and plants all around you looking over a lake of pillows, or like the ocean was putting on a white comforter as a blanket to keep itself warm.

I took a hike that afternoon to a "pond" down the road which was basically just a big puddle and then hung at my campsite until sunset. The people at the campsite next to me were a lovely couple, Zach and Pam, and their dog, Kona. Kona was a funny little dog with a lot of demons inside of him, as he wasn't that friendly to anyone, but I enjoyed having him around. Zach and Pam were probably in their early thirties, and he was a doctor and she was an engineer. They had one of those tents that goes on top of your car and you climb a ladder up in to. I feel like these types of things had seen a huge growth in sales and competition in the past few years as camping and travelling became more and more popular. It gave them an even higher up spot for an even better view than what us peasants on the ground floor had to get. I was a fan of it, and I was a fan of theirs.

They were truly sweet people and we sat out there for a couple hours, cutting it up while watching the sun go down. They were drinking cold beers from their cooler, and I was drinking ice cold Refreshes and munching a ten out of ten tuna sando from mine.

I can honestly say that it was the best sunset I've ever seen. It set so much later than the usual San Diego sunsets because of the whole latitude thing, but also it seemed to go down in slow motion. I was getting the beach colors reflecting off of the water, plus the cloud colors reflecting off the tops of the lake of pillows, plus the silhouettes of the trees bursting through the horizon. The breeze was blowing a little bit and the temperatures had dropped so that it was nice and cool, but not cold.

The weather was perfect, the view was perfect, and the company, which I did not expect to have, was perfect. After the sunset, I opened up all the windows to hear all the sounds that a Big Sur night had to offer and to get the cross breeze like you get at a beach house after a hot day. I hopped up into the truck and read a little bit with my book light before passing out. It was the first time I was really able to read back there. The point of living in the truck was never to be spending a bunch of time in there so when I was going to bed or going "home" I was going to sleep and that was it. So, that night, with nothing but the peaceful sounds of Big Sur and only Zack and Pam, who I am sure would not mind, to see the book light shining through my truck window, I was totally relaxed. I have to say spending some time in the place I had called home for 8 months and getting to enjoy my book was really pleasant. I didn't have to worry about anyone seeing my nightly hop in there and worry that they were going to call the cops on me. I had slept well in the months that I lived in the truck, but that night was the best night of sleep that I can ever remember.

The next morning as I got up from my peaceful slumber, I pulled back the side of the shades to see what kind of day I was waking up to. I was hoping that when I pulled back the shades,

I was going to see the Pacific in all her glory as the very first thing to start my day. The window was all fogged up, so I knew that my ideal morning wasn't going to happen and it was going to be more clouds. Even though it made for a fire of a sunset, I wanted the clouds gone in the morning to wake up to the thing I love the most in this world. I was bummed.

I popped open the shell. Fuck, was I wrong! I couldn't have pictured this view in my head or in a movie any better than what it was. BIG BLUE, all her glory, no clouds. My jaw actually dropped. I get the saying now. I was so excited, I almost had a tear in my eye. I sat there for a few minutes just staring, fixated on this view that I knew would be the most spectacular view I could ever wake up to with the least bullshit around it. Nobody was around taking pictures or talking or doing anything to take away from my moment with Big Blue. The only thing I could see when the shell was popped open was the ocean and the hillside leading down to it. I mean, how many kids my age can say that they owned oceanfront property?

I had a big day planned, so I stayed for about a half hour taking it all in, wrote Zack and Pam a note thanking them for being so friendly and wishing them well for the rest of their trip, and then headed back down the bumpy dirt roads, back towards civilization. More clouds started to roll in as I was making the drive down, so again, I was driving above the clouds, blasting Springsteen, getting mentally prepared for the surf, feeling like a million bucks.

First stop: surfing at Sand Dollar Beach. From everything I had read, this was one of the more forgiving breaks, so I could get after it out there without worrying I was going to get swept under and nobody to come and save my kook ass if need be. I walked down a little, rock filled path to get down to the water and when I got there, it was just me. An empty lineup is something you usually dream of, but I wasn't as stoked about it there. Right before I left, my buddy Chof told me, "Be careful. It's super sharky up there." Even though I already knew as much, it was one of those out of sight, out of mind things until Chof spoke it into reality. As I paddled out, my ears are just ringing of, "It's super sharky up there. It's super sharky up there. It's super sharky up there." I could catch a weird glance off of a wave and think the water was a shark fin. In other words, everything was a shark.

Although Chof's little caveat hampered the beginning of the session, overall it was a fun time. The view couldn't get much better with cliffs on one side and other rocks shooting out of the middle of the water, high into the air like a skyscraper in the ocean, on the other side. The waves were a little choppy and conditions weren't ideal, but the size was decent, so I was able to catch a couple of fun ones. As I got out of the water and headed towards the trail to get back to my truck, an older Asian gentleman tourist looked at me like I had seven heads and said with a slight accent, "You surf out there?!"

I smiled and said that I did and it was fun, he should try it. He looked at me and just said, "ohhhh!!" but his eyes said, "No. It's super sharky out there."

From there, it was a day of touristy stuff. I saw most of the best sights in Big Sur, taking in the coastline of hills on my right and ocean on my left the whole way. I saw a couple of waterfalls, Limekiln and Mcway, the latter looked like a scene straight out of heaven with bright blue water falling from the cliff right into white sand on the beach. Limekiln also had some kilns which were pretty neat to see and since I had nothing else to do while I was there I figured I would check them out. My last sight out of there was the Bixby Bridge. It was going over this long pass with nothing above it, like the Chesapeake Bay Bridge had, to support it. It was a pretty remarkable piece of architecture.

The next stop on the adventure was a quick little pit stop in Santa Cruz and this was a hugely important stop because this was where I was going to take my first shower of the trip that was not in the ocean. It was the only stop along the way with a trusty, dusty 24 Hour Fitness. I didn't even pretend to go in there for a workout, and I think once they saw me and smelled me, they probably didn't even want me to workout, just to get my ass into the shower. Once I was squeaky clean, I went to a bar to watch the Celtics lose again in Game 7 to the Cavs, and ultimately lose the series. The beer was smooth and the food was a nice and warm change of pace from tuna or turkey sandos, so all things considered the night was enjoyable. I had parked in a backstreet of Santa Cruz in a neighborhood of houses that looked like somewhere that I would love to live. Once the C's lost and I watched the sunset on the beach in SC, I was exhausted from all the hiking and the IPAs, so I hopped into the back when I saw that nobody was around and watching me crawl in there. It wasn't as peaceful of a night as it was in Big Sur, but I got a nice shower out of it and another in the morning, so it was the ideal midway point from Big Sur to my final destination of Half Moon Bay.

The trip up to this point could not have worked out better, besides the Celtics losing, obviously. Now, I was moving up in the world and getting a night out of my pickup truck and in a Ritz Carlton hotel room that goes for 900 bucks a night. When I pulled up, there were Ferraris, Porsches, and every other brand of nice car that you could imagine. Somewhere in that same parking lot would be my dusty Toyota Tahoma covered in a weekend's worth of camping and offroading. These people and I were not exactly alike, but you'd have to be a spoiled piece of shit not to enjoy yourself here, no matter who you are.

It always amazed me how miserable some rich people could be. I'm not saying all wealthy people are like this, but I had noticed that there truly wasn't a direct correlation between wealth and happiness. The cliché had held true in my experience. A few months earlier, I had met my old man in Park City for a ski trip. We stayed in a nice hotel, but there was an even nicer one in town that he wanted to go get a drink at. My dad had worked in and for hotels his whole life and was always interested in luxury hotels and seeing how they operated. We got to the hotel and bought ourselves a round of beers at the bar that had the whole mountain as the backdrop. It was a five star hotel for a reason and we were loving every minute of it. I looked around, though, and noticed that we had to have been the only people in that whole bar that were smiling. The rest of the people in there looked like they were having the worst time. We were a wealthy family too, but some of the people that were as wealthy or wealthier than us seemed to take too many of these experiences for granted far too often. One thing that I always admired about both of my parents was their ability to have a ball, whether they were drinking beers at a place like this or at the most divey little roadside bar. I tried to take that same mentality with me, too.

Just because I was homeless and loved eating simple delights like cheeseburgers didn't mean I had denounced all things fancy. Some of those "boujee" things are a blast every now and then, even for a man of simple tastes. So going from the Taco Life for a few days, with camping in the outdoors or in someone's neighborhood and showering at the gym, I had earned a few days of living like a one percenter. That's exactly what Sock and I did for those next couple of days. We drank fine wine, which I almost never do. We golfed 18 on the most, or second most behind Torrey Pines, insane golf course that I had ever played on. I am an absolute hack at golf, but it was still an unbelievable day out there. We didn't exactly treat the course like the normal 1%, though. We snuck our beers onto the course and covered them with the towel when the cart girl would go by. We paid twelve bucks for all of our beers that day rather than twelve bucks per beer, so I was still the average Joe in that regard. We ate incredible steak at the classy restaurant in the hotel. I even walked around the hotel in a robe, really taking advantage of every single perk that the resort had to offer.

Most of all, we looked like the happiest couple in the whole place. Don't get me wrong, Sock and I are so close and bicker so much that we look like a couple often, but this weekend was extreme. We just don't happen to be gay, but when we showed up to this exquisite hotel, drinking our wine and laughing our asses off at all sorts of nonsense, people were naturally going to give us some kind smiles and even a "congratulations" here and there.

Two days and one night at the Ritz later, it was time to get back to my real life, and that was just fine. I had gotten my fix of the finer things in life with heavenly beds and plush robes and was ready to go back to sleeping diagonally in my underoos. As I'm rearranging my surfboard and golf bags into my dusty, dirty, home of a Toyota Tacoma, an older guy in his sixties heading to his Porsche next to me stops and looks at my license plate. He said with a friendly chuckle, "Maryland, huh? You're a long way from home!" I just looked at my out of place truck, with all my belongings and my sleeping quarters in it and a hell of a road trip behind me, and chuckled back and said, "yeah it's been quite the ride." In my head, as I was giving him this George Clooney smirk that said "I know something you don't pal," I was thinking to myself "you have no idea how far off you are, brother. I couldn't be closer to home."

11

MY WAY

(3:12)

I pulled back into San Diego that Wednesday after pit stops in Santa Barbara for surf and Los Angeles for work feeling more refreshed than I ever had from a trip. My car was disgusting, my armpits maybe even worse, but my mind was clear. What I didn't know was how much was about to change over the next coming weeks.

Chof came to me a few days later and told me that the police were starting to crack down on people living in their cars because I guess it had become a problem in our little town. I was happy to hear that it was becoming such a trend, but definitely unhappy to hear that I was going to have to be even more paranoid about the way in which I entered and exited my house on wheels and where I parked it. Chof was born in this town, so he knew all of the ins and outs, so if he was telling me there were whispers of cops cracking down, then I knew it had to be true, and I appreciated his heads up.

It was also getting to the middle of June, so the May Gray of San Diego was starting to die and a heat wave was headed towards us. There were very few instances during the entire time I lived in the truck where I was too hot at night. There were nights where I was cold, but what's better than being cold at night and bundling up into your blankets, rubbing your feet together to get cozy? So, being cold was never a big fear of mine, but I hadn't trucked it through a summer yet, so I was starting to worry a little about what that would look like temperature wise.

Then, I got the worst and best news of all. MC, my brother in arms and the guy I spent most of my time with, was moving back east. It was the worst news because I was losing a guy that, besides the truck living stuff, I could come to about anything and also tear up a rug on the dance floor with out at the bar. He was my right hand man, and nobody was going to be able to replace him out here once he moved. It was the best news though because this was exactly what my guy wanted. He landed his dream job and of all places, they were sending him to Manhattan, his favorite city in the world and right next to his family's hometown. I was genuinely happy for him externally and internally, but deep down I was crushed that a big member of the crew was leaving town for good. It all happened so fast, and he was starting the new gig on July 1.

This also begged the big question, was it finally time to give it up? He had another promotion opportunity back in April and would have had to move to Austin. He assumed that I was going to just seamlessly move into their four bedroom house since I was close with all of those guys and spent a lot of time there with them as it was. Much to his chagrin, I told him that time around that if he got the job, I wasn't ready yet to give up the truck life. I was loving it, especially then since winter was over and I had so much time to be outside, in the water, on my bike, etc. I was glad that I made that decision even though push never came to shove because he didn't get the promotion during that round. April and May, especially with my Memorial Day trip, were some of the best months in there. Now, July was on the horizon, John Law was on the hunt for a fugitive like me, and the heat wave that was looming would make my little box of a home a sauna and have me smelling like a high school locker room every morning hopping out of it. The answer to the question was a bittersweet, "yes, maybe it's time."

I felt in my heart that I had gotten all that I had hoped for and more with the experience. I knew it wouldn't be forever, and candidly, I didn't think it would be this long. I respect the hell out of people that can do it for years. Maybe if my circumstances were different, I could have kept going, but it wasn't about proving a point or making it to a certain amount of time. The experience was about just that, the experience; and goddamn, was it one hell of an experience.

I visited some unreal places: Park City, Breckenridge, Horseshoe Bend, the Grand Canyon, Zion, Huntington Beach, Newport Beach, Laguna Beach, Venice, Lake Tahoe, Santa Barbara, Santa Cruz, Pismo Beach, Grover Beach, Joshua Tree, Anza-Borrego, New York City, Washington, D.C., Half Moon Bay, Big Sur, Anaheim Angels Stadium for a Sox game, STAPLES Center for the Sweet 16, and Tijuana.

Some of those places, like Tahoe and Half Moon Bay, took weeks of planning and preparation and were some of the best weekends of my life. Others, which were sometimes just as memorable and part of the true beauty of the experience, were decided on that day, or sometimes I would just get in the truck and drive straight to my destination without thinking of it at all before. If the waves were shitty in San Diego, I'd take a night trip up to Huntington, crash there, and wake up early and catch cleaner waves there. If none of my friends were doing anything on a Friday, I'd drive out to Anza-Borrego and have a night in the desert under the stars, only to wake up early and catch one of the craziest sunrises I have ever seen. I loved all of those trips, and I loved the guilt free feeling of not paying for a place to stay, the thrill of waking up in the morning feeling like I had beaten the system and was travelling with cheat codes.

I gained about ten pounds of muscle and felt like I was in the best shape of my life. I had made some buddies at the gym and found a morning routine that worked for me. For the most part, I ate pretty healthy, and didn't have to cook at all because I could afford to eat more enjoyable meals every day without paying for rent, and not feel guilty for not cooking them. I didn't look like Brad Pitt from *Troy*, but I liked my progress and could finally do the titty dance with my pecs, so I felt pretty ripped looking in a mirror.

I had gotten significantly better at surfing, yoga, and bike riding… and reading. Now I could probably read at a fourth grade level, but still slow as shit. I surfed some of my favorite waves while living in the truck and surfed way more often than when I was living in a house. I had slowed my mind down with yoga and a little bit of meditation here and there. I could ride my bike from one end of the boardwalk to the other with no hands because I spent so much time on that thing. I read about twice as many books per month as usual… so make it two per month. My little life in the outdoors or practicing a hobby was a hell of a way to live. I didn't need to live in a truck to do it, but I did need to live in the truck to see how much better it was to do it all the time.

It was time, though. I was excited to not worry about anyone seeing my climb into bed. In fact, if anyone saw me climbing into bed while living in a house that would hopefully mean that I would be sleeping with a lovely lady. Now, I would be rooting for someone to see that. I was excited to have roommates to buddy with during the week at all times, but also armed with the new knowledge that I could spend some time alone and enjoy myself. I was excited to start playing my guitar more since there wasn't really a place for me to do it in the truck. And finally, I was excited to start writing some more of this book. I left my laptop in my storage unit, turned off for a full nine months (I was shocked it turned on when I went back to it, so thanks @Apple). So, a lot of this book was actually typed on my iPhone, whether that be at the beach or at the top of Big Sur overlooking the pillowtop clouds with hills poking through them.

I told MC that I'd take over his room, and from then on I started to prep for the end of the era, both with my truck life, my best pal, and my old job because I landed a new, more interesting one in all of this time. Big changes were coming and coming fast. I basically had two more weeks in the truck, so I wanted to make the most of it. I parked at all of my favorite spots in town, with views opening the hatch up to see the ocean or the bay. I spent most of my time in those last few weeks with MC and the boys. We were being a little dramatic, acting as if he was dying, doing all of our old activities, from putt putt to bowling to a going away banger at his old house, my new one, to get in some last good times before our boy headed out.

MC moved on a Friday, so my last night in the truck was a Tuesday night. Wednesday of that week, we all slept in the living room together on the couches and floor swapping stories and laughing over old times. On Thursday I slept on the floor in his room to be close to my guy and bullshit around one last time before I wouldn't see him for six months. So, that Tuesday night, I parked right by the place I parked on that first night, where I ran into the homeless guy all fucked up in the public restroom. It was closure for an era that started with me thinking I was just as crazy as everyone thought I was and that I'd bail on it after day one. The era ended with me waking up with a fat smile on my face that Wednesday morning. I had made it nine months and loved it, and there were really no hiccups along the way. As I would later describe to a friend when he asked how I'd rate the "experiment," it was a ten out of ten.

On Wednesday night I asked my parents to FaceTime me when they could; it was time to tell them too. I always said that I would tell them as soon as it was over, so I had to hold true to my own word. They told me the time they'd be ready for the FaceTime, so I rode my bike down to the beach and got ready for the call. I didn't know what to expect when I told them. I thought my mom would be furious, but my dad would laugh it off and think it was pretty cool.

They picked up the phone, all excited to talk to me and to see FaceTime at work since they were new to it. Their excitement didn't last very long. I told them about the truck and what I wanted to get out of it and how it was now over, but I had gained all I wanted from it and they were stunned.

"You're joking, right?" my mom asked.

"Well… why?" my dad asked, clearly concerned after I said that I wasn't joking.

I tried to explain as best I could, but they still didn't fully get it. My dad was worried that I was afraid to come to him to ask for money. My mom was worried that I was depressed. I sent them a screenshot of my bank account and a video of my Memorial Day Trip that I had put together one day at the laundromat. I was anything but struggling for money, I was saving twice as much per month as I was when I was living in a house. I wasn't the happiest guy in the world, but I for sure wasn't depressed anymore. I had lived my best life for nine months and I learned a lot along the way. The more I explained it, the less upset they got, but none the less confused.

It didn't go as well as I thought, but not as bad as it could have gone either. My mom called me shortly after when it was just her and told me that she was glad that I didn't tell her while I was doing it, but also glad that I enjoyed it and that it sounded so great. I knew my mother well. She said if I told her while I was doing it, she wouldn't have been able to sleep, which was the exact reason I kept that shit to myself, Mama! She also told me that I just needed to give my old man a little time to understand and let it sink in because he was a little worried even now. She always knew how to let me know everything was all right.

Big Dads called me shortly after and knew that I was a little bummed out that he didn't fully understand. He started with telling me that although he didn't understand it, and he probably never would, that he was proud of me as always. This was a saying my old man always told me, whether I had just won the fourth grade basketball championship (on a team he had coached), got a new job or more importantly, any time that I royally fucked up. He wasn't proud of my mistakes, but he always found it important to let me know he was proud of me during those times for everything else. As if to tell me, "this doesn't define you. All the positive things you do define you, so just remember them and find those things, go back to them." I think right then, he didn't know if he was letting me know he was proud of me for the amazing accomplishment that I felt it was or if he was letting me know that, in spite of living in a truck all that time, he was proud of my journey. Really, it didn't matter. He was proud of me, and that was what mattered. He loved me and wanted the best for me and I think he could hear in my voice that I was really doing great, and that was what mattered most to him... even if that meant doing something he thought was absolutely psychotic.

The funny thing was, over those nine months, when I would tell them about all of my experiences, leaving out the detail that I was living in my truck, they were always so excited for me. My mom would always say stuff like, "you're really having an awesome year," or "we are so proud that you're going out and having all of these fun experiences and just living life!"

That was my folks for you. Even if they didn't agree with me, they were always there for me. They always knew that if I thought what I was doing was best for me, they were going to support it as best they could. They understood the truck life perfectly, without understanding the truck part at all. They'd give me advice where they thought necessary and try to steer me in the direction that they thought was best, but ultimately, knew that I was an adult and if I was happy and whole, then so were they. That's why I love that man and woman.

Friday came quicker than I had thought it could, and there I was, waking up in a house for the second night in a row. I woke up on the floor next to my boy, in the bedroom I was about to take over after living in quarters about five percent of that size. MC and I said our goodbyes with some big hugs, choking back tears knowing that we were both about to go through some big changes, the biggest of which being 3,000 miles away from the guy we spent the most of our time with for the past two years. I got into my truck that morning, this time as a vehicle to take me to work, and not my home, and I lost it.

I put on the Lumineers, MC's favorite band and some sad fucking music if you're in that kind of mood, and I just bawled my eyes out for the first twenty minutes of the thirty minute commute. In addition to my boy's move, I was changing homes and changing jobs, and I've never done well with change. I resolved that day to keep living how I had been, keep getting out there, keep surrounding myself with wonderful people like my boy Michael Colello, and keep the man between my own two ears at bay making him my best friend and not my worst enemy. Change was coming, but it was how I was going to handle the change that was going to be the most telling, not the change itself.

I got home from work that day, and all of my new roommates were out of town, the house empty. A note was left for me on my new nightstand, from MC. In it, he wrote a lot of things that he'd miss about our friendship, but then wrote, "There is one thing I absolutely despise about you though. You don't give yourself enough credit. You're a smart guy who is loved dearly by his friends, always a joy to be around, very hardworking, and that beard... are you kidding me? Seriously though your character and the way you handle yourself as a man has taught me a lot and I try every day to be more like PFG." Holy shit, did the waterworks come. MC knew about all the battles that were going on inside of my own head and how hard I worked to push through them and really believed that I shouldn't face them at all. The tough criticism I gave myself that I thought everyone else saw in me too, maybe nobody else did but me.

In this big house, I felt more lonely than I had ever felt living in the truck. I texted an old friend to meet up for a beer to get me out of the house and into that big, not so bad, world. There was more living to be done out there.

In the months since, I've maintained a happy, healthy life. Do I still go to the gym every single day? Do I spend as much time outside, surfing, bike riding, reading? Do I travel as much as I did so happily? The answer was no to all, but I still did a lot of it all. There were times that I would worry that I was happier in there than I am in here, but at the same time, the grass is always greener. I mostly remember all of the good things about the truck because that was what made it valuable and you're always going to have complaints, no matter where you are in your life and in your living situation.

Mostly, I was happy in my new home. I had great roommates, I had a running shower, I had a bed that I could lay in not diagonally (to be honest, I often find myself waking up diagonally in the middle of the night). Life was good, and what was most important was that I had that knowledge of what I was missing when I was unhappy. Now, I knew when I was in my ruts, not to spend it wallowing, but to spend it thriving. Just because I now had an excuse to wallow, didn't mean that I should. I'm trying my best to live that healthy, happy life that I was living in the truck and just taking it into the "real world" even though I'm no longer forced outside of that comfort zone.

People often ask me now, "How do you like living in a house?" It is by far my least favorite question. I lived in a house 97% of my life. It wasn't some new frontier to me, and those same people that asked were usually the people that made fun of me while I lived in the truck. So, when they asked it is usually in a patronizing tone. They didn't really care how I was doing in my new abode, they wanted me to show a chink in my armor and admit that I was as stupid as they thought I was the whole time. Do I miss the actual sleeping aspect? No, not at all. It is obviously better to sleep in a home with a real door and a real bed, but I do miss the lifestyle. Yes, I like living in a house, but do I regret living in my truck? Fuck, no. I don't, not even for one second.

A girl I was friends with asked me that very question with a condescending giggle and I responded, "yeah it's got its ups and downs." It was an answer that I don't think was acceptable for her. She wanted me to say how amazing it was compared to living in my awful truck. The truth was there were ups and downs, but she kept pushing.

"Well do you like standing up when you wake up?" she pressed on with questions like this, poking me to try to get me to break, until finally I had to just look her in the eyes and say, "I mean, I don't know what you want me to say? I don't regret doing it at all." To which, she laughed. Some people just will never get it, and that's fine. I wasn't doing it for anyone else. I was doing it for me.

Most people I tell now with pride. I was shy about it while I was living in there because I might have been a little embarrassed, or I just wanted to avoid the conversation because a lot of people wouldn't understand and would just piss me off with the way they'd laugh at me or ask me questions as if I was a science project. Now, I tell people with a smile on my face and usually they are very nice about it. People usually say that they wish they could do it, or that they could never or would never do it, but good for me for doing it. I've found that most people are genuinely good and politely curious about it all. It's a fun little thing to talk about because now people look at it like, "hey he's normal now, living in a house, but that's so cool of him getting out there and trying it."

In the last days of me writing this book in 2019, I was sitting at my desk one day, bored as hell, cleaning out my wallet. I was taking out old receipts when I noticed this yellow thing stuck at the bottom. I reached my index finger in there and tried wiggling it out to no avail for a couple of minutes. After nearly tearing the whole damn wallet apart at the seams, I got this little, yellow, crumpled and folded post-it note out of there. I unfolded it and couldn't help but cheese when I read what it had said.

"2017
Be more positive
Move into truck
Commit to happiness
Think BIG"

I must have written it in January of that year as a resolution and put it in my wallet to hold me accountable. I may not have ever thought about it after that day for the rest of that year, so it didn't consciously hold me accountable. I did, however, definitely move into my truck in 2017… and I think I was able to check off each of the other resolutions for that year as well.

12

CHEESEBURGER IN PARADISE

(2:03)

"394?" Henry asked right as I was sitting down, referring to the light pale ale that had grown to be my favorite beer since moving out to San Diego. More importantly, it was the beer that had come to be my "usual" every time I set foot into my favorite burger joint and dive bar, Sonny's Pub, or to most people just Sonny's.

I gave Henry a nod, trying with all my might to hold back the smile from bursting through at the fact that I was truly a regular here. It had been a couple of months now that I had been recognized and was slowly earning my chops. It started with them knowing my beer, moving up to handshakes when I walked in and then inviting me to the following year's NFL survivor pool that all the bartenders and a few regulars were a part of, and now I really felt like this was my spot. These were my pals. Even so, anytime I got any type of regular acknowledgement, I couldn't help but feel all sorts of juiced on the inside knowing I'd made it.

To most people, being a regular, much less being a regular at a bar, isn't something they would be too proud of. I wear it like a badge of honor. This isn't just some bar. This is the place that you go to wallow in your deepest miseries, but also where you go to celebrate your finest days. It had an "I don't really give a fuck what you think about us, we know we're the best" attitude in there. Kooks were constantly walking in trying to pay with credit card, it is a cash only bar, only to be told such. They always came back with a, "Reallly???" as if cash never existed in the first place. My guys always responded the same way, "Yes... really. ATM outside" and couldn't care less about the customers' disgust that they didn't take cards.

After a few months of going and getting the lay of the land, I decided to bring a girl in there for the first time. She was the first girl I had ever taken to Sonny's for a couple reasons. The first being the place isn't packed with a bunch of chicks. The typical patron of the fine establishment is a bald 37 year old white guy with a bit of a Dad shelf, meaning he can rest his .394 pale ale on his belly when he sits down at the right angle.

To be clear, I get nervous bringing other fellas to Sonny's too, but almost all men like burgers and women can be a bit more picky. Sonny's is not to be confused as an anti-woman place, though, because Sonny herself is a woman. I met her one time because she only worked one day during the week and when I happened to have a random day off on that day, I went in to get my chance to see her. Her legend preceded her, as she was everything that I had pictured to be the owner of a place like that and more. She served the tables as if she was just a regular employee, and when someone came up to ask if she and the other server were in line, she simply replied, "Oh no, we work here. Go ahead." Nothing pretentious or, "Yes, this is my bar" type of attitude, she just acted like she was one of the gang and kept busting her ass like the rest of 'em while eating some Kit Kats. When I was introduced to her I told her that

Sonny's was my favorite spot in the entire world and she could never understand how much I meant that.

The second reason that it was the first time that I had brought a female was I hadn't found one worthy of going in. It was high praise. I was nervous she'd walk in there and order a soda. I had two buddies come in there one time and order Coca-Colas and the bartender looked at me in disappointment and disgust saying, "You know these guys?" It was a pub. You should order beer. That was the last time I ever took someone who didn't have the intention of sucking down a pint with their burger. I also vowed that I'd never go in there without ordering a beer myself. In all the times I had gone hungover and thought about not getting one, I hadn't.

Or worse, I was worried she would ask for a substitute. The place doesn't have menus, per se. It has a chalk board with 5 things written on it:

1/2 pound Cheeseburger
1/2 pound Hamburger
1/3 pound Hamburger
1/3 pound Cheeseburger
Fries

I cringe everytime someone asks some dumbass question like "Do you have hot dogs?" or "Can I get bacon on mine?" It's not even worthy of response if you ask me; it would be like going to a Michelin star restaurant and asking if they have SPAM or fluffernutters for sale. So, finally I had found a girl that I knew wouldn't embarrass me with stupid questions like that. She liked the Allman Brothers Band, Mumford and Sons and barely wore any makeup at all. She was naturally beautiful, what did she need makeup for to fuck up the whole thing she had going? Now I am not saying those two things make a dream girl, but I think that's not a girl that asks for her burger well done with something pretentious like foie gras on it. That seems more like the "PLAY CHAINSMOKERS" the entire pregame kind of girl, the same kind of girl that puts on makeup and curls her hair before going to the gym. A Sonny's girl should be easy going, down to earth, and low maintenance; I had found one just like that.

So I prepped her, she had cash, she was ready to order a beer, she knew better than to ask for a substitute and I didn't even bother prepping her for that one. We got to the door and she handed the bouncer her ID, he looked at it for a bit grilling her and said "I can't take it." She was a pretty small girl and could pass as 22, but not under 21. It was because her ID was horizontal so, legally, they weren't supposed to take them in. That is one thing that you'd think they would be a little lax on, but the ID thing is huge. I guess they think of all the things to screw the whole operation, the last thing they want is for an underage to be in their bar. So we were standing their with our dicks in our hands thinking we were going to have to settle and go get some shitty restaurant across the street when one of the bartenders looked out from behind the bar and told the bouncer to fuck off with a shooing motion and we were fine to get in. We were regulars, he told the bouncer, and again I was on cloud nine; it would never get old.

As we sat down, he said, "Next time you bring in underage girls, make sure you bring enough for all of us. Now, what are you drinkin?" It was one of my favorite visits to Sonny's and the girl I had brought proved that she was worthy of the honor.

Everything about the place was special to me. From the wood paneling throughout the whole place to the signed pictures of famous patrons that had come through, including my favorite of Arnold Palmer flicking off one of his golf buddies by scratching his chin. The thing that always got me coming back in there though was the burgers. No fancy shmancy BS, just lettuce, tomato, onion, meat, cheese and mayo on the most perfect bun there was.

It must have been once every third time going in there that I'd say, "now this. This one is the best yet." And every time I really meant it.

Once you had gotten your fill, there was no better feeling in the world than the three seconds right when you walked out. Sonny's was pretty dark for the most part so when you walked out you were immediately hit by sunlight or streetlight from the lamps above. With a belly full of ice cold beer and the greatest burger around, I can honestly say I could not imagine being more satisfied than feeling that plus the sunshine hitting my face. I imagine I look like Andy Dufresne, when he's driving down that coastal highway after he busts out of jail, and has that little smile on his face that seems to be his face's new natural state. At that moment, I feel like the embodiment of content.

All that and more is what brought me there on a spring night while I was living in the truck. I had an absolute butt cheeks day at work and I needed something wonderful in my life and in my belly. The only way to get to Sonny's in my mind was by walking, so that's what I did. It was an easy stroll and along the bay for the most part, so by the time I got there I had forgotten about why I was in such a bad mood and was ready to just unwind with my old pals, the Sonny's crew.

Sometimes when you walk in, the place is absolutely packed, and that held true that night. But you can usually get pretty lucky and find a spot after a standing beer, which was also true on that night. Usually, one of the guys would point to a seat for me when I got in there to say who was close to finishing up, so that I could linger around there until they got up. I got the very best spot in the bar. The corner seat, opposite the biggest TV. I settled in next to two married ladies and their guy friend on my right, and two guy buddies on my left. They were both fantastic groups of people.

This was another one of the things I saw a huge change in in my time living in the truck. I'm still pretty shy, but before the truck life, I wouldn't be nearly as likely to go to a bar alone and chat up strangers. Now, it had become one of my most enjoyable activities. Whether alone in a bar in Tahoe or alone in a bar in your own hometown, there will usually be someone with enough goodness in them to chat you up and include you in some laughs. Either that, or there will almost always be someone with enough beers in them to chat you up. That night at Sonny's, I had both.

The ladies to my right complimented my hair and said I looked like Bradley Cooper. It was pre-A Star is Born, where I had been told my long hair and beard were similar to Jackson Maine's, so I hadn't heard that one yet. I wasn't going to argue with them, though. BC is a stud! The ladies had gotten married pretty recently and were giving me tips on how to meet a woman of my own. Ultimately, they told me what I had already known. There wasn't going to be a secret spot or formula on where to go or what to do to meet the one. Just keep being yourself and the right one will eventually land in your lap when you aren't expecting it. Like these two, when one was looking for some drugs when she was in her early twenties at a party, and the other happened to be the one at the party that had some. Since then, they had fallen in love and had an amazing relationship that was tangible in just a matter of minutes.

To my left was a big guy and his best friend since middle school both out for some beers on their night off from the kids, while their wives patiently waited at home. They told me stories about their kids and their marriages.

Their best story was about how they had planned on having a nice dinner, the two of them and their two wives, last New Year's Eve up in the mountains. The two best pals since middle school thought the only way to drink all day was to start in the morning, so they got absolutely wasted and didn't even make it to the dinner, a story I knew all too well when me and my buddies got together.

When my burger got there, I readied myself for the battle the same way as each time before. It was a ritual I loved to complete and took pride in doing.

The burgers and fries came on a yellow sheet of paper in one of those plastic, red baskets with the holes. One of my first times in there, I saw a local legend take the yellow paper out of the basket, with the burger and fries still on top. He then rested the yellow paper flat onto the table turning the entree from a cramped jacuzzi with too many people in the water to an Infiniti pool with each patron having plenty of room to operate. I mean, there was a lot of room to dip your fries and manhandle your burger. When I saw the old guy do this, I knew I'd never eat mine from the basket ever again. I hadn't.

The next step was to take a little bit of the pepper juice that came in these little brown jars filled with spicy peppers. I'd take a spoon and dunk it in so that the juice would flow on top of it and then slowly pull it out and drizzle the sweet nectars all over my fries to give them a little kick. This was a trick I had picked up from another local and I did it the same day and the fries had never tasted better. I knew I'd never eat my Sonny's fries without the juice again. I hadn't.

The big guy was astonished. He had never seen anything like it. He was acting like I was Russel Brand in *Forgetting Sarah Marshall* and he was the guy that had never had sex before. I had all the answers and he was the novice. We geeked over how excited he was about it and I told him that I was the exact same way the first time I had seen these little tricks.

He looked at his buddy and said, "We've *got to* get another now." They had already eaten a half pounder and fries, but now that they had seen the best way to eat it, they wanted nothing more than to do one like that. They ordered seconds, a move I had never seen at Sonny's and we all belly laughed some more and ordered more rounds of beers.

I went back and started talking to the married ladies some more and we got to talking about where they were from and where I was from.

"Maryland?" one of them said, "That's a long way from home. What, were you running from something?"

I knew many of my friends from home probably knew the answer to this. There were even more people that knew better than to come out and ask me, even if they didn't know why I had moved all the way out to California and then eventually into my truck. But that was the truth. I was running from something.

I was running from a job I'd hate only to come home to a couch and watch TV until I had to go to bed and only live for the weekend. Too many of my friends from back east complained about that exact type of lifestyle and it freaked me out. I didn't want to live that life once I graduated from college, so I chose to live in sunny San Diego. I was running to a place I could get home from work and surf or ride my bike along the beach and watch sunsets every night of the week, but still look forward to a hell of a weekend.

I was running from a toxic girl that broke my heart and made me lose all confidence in myself. I was running from my low self esteem ever since she had pulled me back in time and time again only to find different things that were wrong with me and remind me of my shortcomings. I was running to find the next woman that would want me to just be me and laugh at my jokes, just as I could laugh at hers. I was running from the fact that all my best friends had found all this already, and I was failing again and again.

"Actually... yeah" was my answer to the woman sitting next to me and it was the first time I had really admitted it to myself let alone to anyone else; although, I'm sure others had known it. The truth was I was still running. I was running from different things now than what I had ran from when I moved to California. Now, I was literally living as a man on the run, on the road, on the backstreets. But at this time in my life, I had felt more so than in a long time that I was close to being still. I was happy with where I was, I was happy with the skills I had gained, the books I had read, and the things I had learned about myself. I was able to run but be content by myself and be a friend to my own mind. I had gotten so much peace of mind from the time I spent with just me, enjoying the things I had always enjoyed but was too lazy to seek out often enough, instead of wallowing in my sorrows in my room thinking of all of my mistakes and missteps over the years.

I had also gotten peace of mind meeting people I would have never met. From Terry in Tahoe to the married ladies next to me, my shy ass probably never would have struck up conversation with them had I been spending all this time in the comfort of being with my roommates all the time.

I won't say that everything was fixed and that my anxiety had come to a complete stop and I had found all the answers. Of course, I still had my issues, still worried here and there, but much less. I was comfortable enough and I was in a beautiful place in my life.

She responded after a small pause "yeah, who isn't?" in a friendly, upbeat way that really stuck with me. She said it as if all the people that said they had it all figured out were full of shit and in some way or another we were all metaphorically living in our trucks. We were all doing something to push ourselves into situations we wouldn't necessarily be in otherwise, to find what we were really looking for. For me, what I was really looking for was to be happy with what I had and spend more time for me and I had found a lot of that.

In that moment, as I looked to my left I saw the big guy polishing off burger and fry number two and thanking me for showing him the way to do Sonny's right. All along my journey I had so many moments like this with strangers. Moments that I cherish knowing that by running and searching for some answers to my biggest worries, I would find some of them and find some keys to my own happiness. I was again the picture of serenity talking to these fine people with varying conversations. One group I had just taught how to properly drizzle their fries with pepper juice and had them thinking I had found all the answers. I hadn't.

I had just gotten a weight off of my chest with the other group. I told them how I was running from something, which basically meant how I used to have this mental block in me that wouldn't allow me to be happy by just being alone and just get out of my own head. They probably wondered if I had worked through some of it and had finally stopped the running, of both mind and body. I polished off my pint, walked out of the pub and into the light, felt that contentment once again and knew then, I had.

— END —

NOTES

1. McClusky, Mark. *Faster, Higher, Stronger: How Sports Science Is Creating a New Generation of Superathletes - and What We Can Learn from Them*. Hudson Street, 2014

2. Feldman, Lucy. "Van Life: Live in Your Van, Post on Instagram." *Time*, Time, 6 Oct. 2017, time.com/hashtag-van-life-people-live-in-vans/.

3. Reed, Chris. *Commentary: More Californians Living in Cars? A 'Wheel Estate' Boom Is Coming*. San Diego Union-Tribune, 28 Dec. 2017, www.sandiegouniontribune.com/opinion/sd-living-in-cars-in-california-20171227-story.html.

4. Weisman, Aly. "The Incredible Story Of How Chris Pratt Got His Big Break While Living In A Scooby Doo Van In Maui." *Business Insider*, Business Insider, 19 Aug. 2014, www.businessinsider.com/chris-pratt-lived-in-a-van-before-he-was-famous-2014-8.

5. Hoffower, Hillary. "California Real Estate Is so Expensive That Families, Retirees, and Even Tech Workers Are Living in Cars and Vans." *Business Insider*, Business Insider, 21 Aug. 2018, www.businessinsider.com/california-housing-so-expensive-people-live-in-cars-vans-2018-8.

6. Becker, Joshua. *The More of Less: Finding the Life You Want Under Everything You Own*. Waterbrook, 2018.

7. Smith, Daniel B. *Monkey Mind: A Memoir of Anxiety*. Simon & Schuster, 2013.

8. Robinson JP & Martin S. What do happy people do? *Social Indicators Research*, December 2008 DOI: <u>10.1007/s11205-008-9296-6</u> - Robinson & Martin

9. Murray, Krystina. "Homelessness and Addiction." *AddictionCenter*, 19 Nov. 2018, www.addictioncenter.com/addiction/homelessn ess/.

10. Rogan, Joe. "#975 - Sebastian Junger." *The Joe Rogan Experience*, vol. 975, 9 June 2017.

11. Potts, Rolf. *Vagabonding: an Uncommon Guide to the Art of Long-Term World Travel*. Ballantine Books, 2016.

12. Kumar, A., Killingsworth, M. A., & Gilovich, T. (2014). Waiting for Merlot: Anticipatory Consumption of Experiential and Material Purchases. *Psychological Science*, *25*(10), 1924– 1931. <u>https://doi.org/10.1177/0956797614546 556</u>

13. Ferriss, Timothy. *Tools of Titans: the Tactics, Routines, and Habits of Billionaires, Icons, and World-Class Performers*. Houghton Mifflin Harcourt, 2017.

14. Tropper, Jonathan. *This Is Where I Leave You*. Dutton, a Member of Penguin Group (USA) Inc., 2014.

ACKNOWLEDGEMENTS

I cannot thank the people who made all of this possible enough. Thank you to Jesse Schwartz who edited it like nobody else could have: by telling me what sucked and what nuggets were good. Thank you to Dillon Glenn for the cover design, putting in the work above and beyond and creating a cover that my unartistic ass could have never even envisioned in my own mind, let alone create. Thank you to Wesley Horbatuck IV who was always a big fan of my creative process and motivated me to keep pushing this thing along even when I had my moments of doubt and for taking the photo of me that is on the back cover. Thank you to the greatest artist to ever live, Mr. Bruce Springsteen, whose music has helped me get through some of the toughest times and made the best times even better. "Backstreets" is a favorite song of mine; so, if by some miracle this book should ever find you, I hope you take the title as an homage and not a poor use of the name. Lastly and most importantly, thank you to all of my friends and family who stuck with me during this time even when they thought I was a lunatic. I hope this helps you better understand the way my mind works and why I enjoyed the journey so much. Cheers to many more journies to come. Happy hunting. Always trying to get home.

-PFG

Made in the USA
Middletown, DE
25 May 2021

40420993R00104